AGAINST THE ODDS

A STORY OF COURAGE, FAITH AND RESOLVE

SALEEM A. KHAN, M.D.

WITH LOVE, RESPECT

Saleem A. Khan, MD

5/08/2023

Library of Congress Control Number: 2023905061

ISBN Print: 979-8-9877873-4-2

ISBN eBook: 979-8-9877873-5-9

CONTENTS

DEDICATION

To my father, Musahib-Ud-Din and my mother Wazir Begum, for teaching me the value of education, love for family and the virtue of helping others.

QUOTES

"Whoever directs someone to do good will gain the same reward as the one who does good."

Hadith of the Prophet Muhammed (Peace Be Upon Him)

❧❧❧❧❧ ❦❦❦❦❦

"Life's most persistent and urgent question is, what are you doing for others?"

Dr. Martin Luther King, Jr.

ADVANCE PRAISE FOR AGAINST THE ODDS

"Treat yourself to an inspiring story of a bright young man who was determined to climb out of poverty and to help others acquire a better standard of living. It is a story about grit, strength, and faith, and how one person's actions can have a beautiful ripple effect that extends far beyond oneself."

– The Reverend Gregory Knox Jones, Senior Minister of Westminster Presbyterian Church in Wilmington, Delaware and the author of *Play the Ball Where the Monkey Drops It: Why We Suffer and How We Can Hope.*

"An inspirational story of how hard work and hope can prevail over distance, time, and partitions, and how from family to roadside fruit stands to meeting a president, the selflessness and commitment of one humble man in Pakistan helped to plant seeds -- in the ground, and in people's

3

SALEEM A. KHAN, M.D.

hearts -- that continue to bloom all around the world and will bring nourishment and prosperity for generations to come."

- Bryan Townsend, Majority Leader, Delaware State Senate

"This motivational biography is a fascinating look at the history of Pakistan through the eyes of a brilliant scientist. I am thoroughly impressed by Professor Musahib-UD- Din Khan's dedication to education and service to his country. His work has had a significant impact on the lives of thousands of people. He is a true role model not only for our generation but for future generations too. I strongly recommend that you read this book and benefit from Professor Khan's insight, knowledge and years of experience."

– Belal BMA, President of the Islamic Society of Delaware

"Through a compelling, well written narrative on the life of a legend, Professor Khan's inspiring story about his struggle to get an education is told. From a modest background, he became an authority on agriculture, which is powerful evidence that positive change begins with education and that education is the key to address all problems"

– Arif Gafur, President, The Citizens Foundation, USA

"Although written as a biography of one of the most consequential scientists in Pakistan's early history, the outpouring of love makes it read like a love story; love of a son for his father, love of a great-grandchild for her

4

great-grandfather; love for education; love for excellence; love for research; and love for uplifting the poor farmers' economic conditions and It is the kind of love story we all need to learn from."

—Naveed Baqir, PhD, Member: Board of Education, Christina School District, New Castle County, Delaware

"Professor Khan's story is an inspiration to all who are struggling to make their dreams come true. It is a reminder that no matter how difficult the situation may be, with perseverance, anything is possible. His dedication and hard work paid off, and he was able to make a difference in the lives of many people in his home country. He set up a good example to follow."

– Dr. Amna Latif, Principal and Director: Tarbiyah School

"This book is an excellent effort to highlight the salient contributions of Professor Khan, who worked hard to mitigate poverty among farmers by introducing them to modern agricultural techniques and fertilizers in the considerably populated developing country of Pakistan. He also encouraged young scientists to perform research and develop better varieties of many different crops, in his mission to make his country self-sustainable in basic edibles and to ensure food security for his people."

– Dr. Abdul Rahman Khan, Principal Scientist (Horticulture), Nuclear Institute for Agriculture and Biology (NIAB) Faisalabad, Pakistan

SALEEM A. KHAN, M.D.

"The story of Musahib-Ud-Din Khan, an internationally- known specialist in horticulture, was written by his son, Dr Saleem Khan with the help of his family. The book is a treasure not only for his descendants but for all faced with unexpected situations. The traumatic experiences this family lived through during and after the 1947 British partition of India, shows us that with faith and focus all things are possible. "

-Kim Burdick, Historian; Author of Revolutionary Delaware: Independence in the First State

"Dr. Saleem Khan's love for his beloved father, the late Professor Musahib-Ud-Din Khan, shines forth on every page of this book. We learn the experiences – both brutal and inspiring -- on both sides of the India-Pakistan partition of 1947. As a spiritual leader in the Jewish faith, I was especially appreciative of Dr. Khan's descriptions of daily Muslim practice – not of an Imam, but of a humble scientist, who lived an observant life. And I learned as much from Dr. Saleem Khan's grandmother, Fazalunissa's practice, as I did from our protagonist."

-Rabbi Michael S. Beals, President, Delaware Association of Rabbis and Cantors; Gubernatorial-Appointed Chair, Delaware Council of Faith-Based Partnerships; Senior Rabbi, Congregation Beth Shalom of Wilmington, Delaware

AGAINST THE ODDS

Professor Musahib Ud Din Khan
Photo Courtesy of Ayub Institute

FOREWORD

As a lifelong Delawarean, I know how special it is to call our state home. People from around the world come to Delaware, *The First State*, to create a better life for themselves and their families. Such is the case with Dr. Saleem Khan, child and adolescent psychiatrist, philanthropist, and community leader who has made Delaware his residence for nearly four decades. Whether an international policy forum or community event or Ramadan dinner, I can always count on Dr. Khan to be present with me. His sincere kindness expressed to all with his smile and eagerness to assist no matter the need or case, makes him a friend to all. Therefore, I was honored when he asked me to share my thoughts about his inspirational father, Professor Musahib-Ud-Din Khan's story.

Professor Khan was a man who traveled across the world in pursuit of education. I know how much a degree can mean to an individual who is looking for a way out of poverty. My own grandmother quit school at an early age to work on the family farm, limiting her options to help provide for her family. Throughout his life, Dr. Khan's father exemplifies how to use the power of education to broaden his horizons, eventually achieving high-level government positions and a wealth of knowledge that was passed down through generations.

Dr. Khan hopes that this book will serve as an inspiration to those who are just beginning life's journey. By reading about young people who were discouraged from pursuing higher education, he hopes to encourage everyone to invest in themselves by going to college. In my position as Lieutenant Governor, it is my hope that all Delawareans are given the opportunity to follow in Musahib-Ud-Din's footsteps and pursue higher education should they choose to do so. The ability to forge your own path is priceless, and the most direct route is through education. Though Professor Khan faced many challenges in his years on this earth, he survived them all with singular determination. In Delaware we celebrate his descendants as they are building their own communities across the Country, including the First State's own, Dr. Saleem Khan.

We are richer as a state, nation and global community thanks to the efforts of Musahib-Ud-Din and his family and those he mentored. This book provides key lessons for each of us to apply everyday in order to uplift current and future generations.

Bethany Hall-Long PhD, RN; Lt Governor of Delaware; Professor, University of DE

PREFACE

As a child, I observed that my dad was always busy with his work, preparing his lectures and marking test papers. Most evenings, his senior students would visit him at our home to discuss their research projects. He would often go on long walks with us and observe all different crops in his experimental fields.

He told my siblings and me how he grew up during British rule. As an Indian boy, he felt discouraged from working toward a college education. According to Dad, the rulers wanted Indians to stop after high school and start working to help the day-to-day operations of the government.

Also, his family was poor and had no money to afford his college education. As he tried to solicit financial help, he faced rejections again and again. He felt all the doors were closing on him and he had no one to turn to. Dad faced all the challenges with courage and complete faith in Allah (God) but never gave up.

Throughout his professional life, he dealt with many challenging situations and turned them all into opportunities. In his personal life, he went out of his way to help many family members, who managed to escape from India to their new homeland of Pakistan.

One day when he was visiting me in the US, I had a heart to heart talk with him. I asked him how he was able to persevere against all odds. His answer was, "Son, I always believe that Allah (God) helps those who try their best and remain patient."

After listening to him, I said, "Dad, I am very proud of you. One day I am going to write a book about you encouraging family, friends and even strangers to learn from the incredible story of your life."

I saw tears of gratitude in Dad's eyes when he gave me a big hug and made a comment, "May Allah always keep you happy and healthy, and give you strength to keep helping others."

A few months after his visit to the US, Dad passed away. His passing made my determination to write this book even stronger. I hope this inspirational book reaches many readers and they are convinced that with courage, faith and resolve, anything is possible.

***

My Deepest Gratitude Goes Out To...

First of all, I thank Allah, who gave me the patience to do the extensive research needed to gather all the necessary information for this important undertaking.

I am thankful to members of my family for encouraging me as I was working on the most valuable project in my life. My special thanks to my older sister Naeem for discussing every little detail with me almost on a daily basis over a long period of time and providing helpful feedback.

I would like to thank Dr Habib-Ur-Rehman, for reading the first manuscript of the book and writing down helpful comments. Whenever I needed a consultation related to agricultural sciences, I contacted him and Dr. Abdul Rahman Khan. They both gladly helped me.

My granddaughter Usma Lateef has certainly earned my respect for writing a heartwarming introduction to this book. I am also very appreciative of my granddaughter Anisa Lateef for doing the last proofreading and making several worthwhile suggestions.

I feel honored that Lt. Governor Bethany Hall-Long wrote the foreword and Professor Muqtedar Khan endorsed the book by writing "A message of hope" (back cover).

I feel indebted to my editor, Gretchen Elhassani. Without her ongoing involvement, it would have been very difficult for me to complete this book. Together we were able to document the amazing life story of a hardworking, sincere and benevolent man, my beloved dad.

I hope this book becomes an inspiration to those who face hardships in their lives and do not have the means to complete their desired education. I also hope that once they read this book, they are convinced that, like Dad, they too can turn challenges into opportunities and achieve their worthy goals.

Saleem A. Khan, M.D.

INTRODUCTION

In fourth grade, I had to do a project on my family lineage and was instructed to bring family heirlooms to class. Our family doesn't have anything passed down, so I felt dejected upon seeing my classmates bring in objects that were passed down in their families for generations. But then I remembered my grandpa, who is the author of this book, telling me about his father and his achievements. Thus, I did research on my great-grandfather, printed the cover of his book out, and prepared some points about him.

When it came to presentation day, the parents were fascinated by my table even though there were just papers and no family heirlooms. I told them how my great-grandfather discovered that beta carotene was found in grapefruits and how he helped Pakistan with his research on kinnows, even though I didn't really know what that meant at the time.

Five years later, I can finally fully understand the impact my great-grandfather had on my grandpa's life and the lives of many others, when my grandpa told us more about his father. I learned that his father had made important discoveries in horticultural sciences, which coincidentally is a field that I am thoroughly intrigued by and plan to study in college.

In the summer of 2019, my family and I took a trip to San Francisco. Per my request, we visited UC Berkeley since I knew that my great-grandfather attended the school. I was enthralled by every corner of the campus, knowing that my great-grandfather had been there many years ago. Once my grandpa heard about our excursion, he immediately requested to have a few copies of his father's certificate from the university sent to him; one of them is framed and sitting on my desk after my grandpa gifted it to me.

Even though my great-grandfather didn't have the money to afford college, he found ways to pursue his education and succeed nonetheless. With courage, faith, and resolve, my great- grandfather excelled against the odds. People are still benefitting today from his research and discoveries, which were made possible due to his raw hard work and determination.

It is certainly an honor to introduce a book about my great-grandfather, *Against the Odds: A Story of Courage, Faith, and Resolve.*

Usma Lateef

Chapter One

Against the Odds

It was still dark when she woke up. As always, Fazalunissa gently reminded herself there was work to be done. Casting off the blankets, she rose. Slippers anticipated her feet beside the bed. They made no sound as she walked quietly across the room, closing the door behind herself so as not to wake her husband.

She could hear the donkeys plodding down the road in the early morning, carrying their loads into town. A rooster crowed, followed by a few others, like a choir heralding the dawn.

She poured water into a metallic jug and began her wudu (ablution), in preparation for the morning prayer. She was used to doing this ritual of purification five times a day. Hands first, then water cupped from one palm into her mouth. She finished by washing her feet, relishing the chill of the liquid between her toes.

After the wudu was completed, she spread her prayer mat out on the floor in the same place it always went. As usual, she faced the Qibla (direction required by Muslim prayers).

"Allah Ho Akbar (God is the greatest)," she whispered. After that, she recited two Surahs, (chapters) Surah, Al-Fatiha (first surah of the Quran) and surah, *Al Ikhlas*, translated as "There Is Only One God." She bent, lowered her head to the floor and completed her prayer, just as she did every morning.

After the prayer, there was bread to be made. She sat down on a small stool, put some wheat flour in a deep bowl, added a couple of cups of water, and started kneading the dough. The sun was rising above the fields. From the kitchen window, she could now see the leaves of the mango tree in her front yard. The road beyond was empty, but it would soon fill with children going to school and men biking to work.

She was preoccupied when her husband Sher Muhammed entered the kitchen. "Assalamu alaikum (Peace be with you)," he said. Fazalunnisa jumped. The bowl skittered away, but she was able to catch it by stretching her arm out far, fingers thick with dough. When her husband noticed that, right away he tried to comfort her.

It was time for him to go to work. As a senior teacher, he was always the first one to reach the school building and unlock doors so that staff and students could get in. He had been doing that for many years at the administration's request.

He was about to put water on for tea when Fazalunissa said, "I had that dream again."

She continued preparing breakfast as she waited for his response. It was clear to him that she wanted an answer. "Tell me again, what was the dream?" he asked her.

"I saw two roses, one of them beautiful and bright red."

"Did you see two names written on the ceiling?" he asked.

"I never went to school, and I cannot read. What are the names?" She wanted to know.

"Musahib and Misbah," he replied.

She came very close to him, her pregnant belly protruding beneath her housedress. "Do you know what this dream means?"

"We are having twins," he said, smiling up at her.

"Twins?" she asked.

"Yes. Allah (God) is going to bless us with two boys. I would like to name them Musahib and Misbah. These names have excellent meanings. I hope you like them too."

"But what about the roses?" She wanted to touch her belly but her hands were still mired in flour and water.

"One of our twins will be a famous man one day," Sher Muhammed responded. "Like the beautiful and bright red rose you have seen in your dream."

"We are poor people. How will our child become famous?" she asked her husband.

Sher Muhammed looked into her eyes confidently and spoke, "Our Creator gives respect or disgrace to whomever He wants."

She knew he was right. Her husband was a spiritual man; he would be able to interpret dreams. "Alhamdulillah (Thank God)," she whispered.

CHAPTER TWO

MUSLIM FAMILY IN INDIA

Musahib-Ud-Din was born in 1917 to a Muslim family in India under British rule. Muslims had been in India since the 600s, the time of the Prophet Muhammad, peace be upon him (PBUH).

In the seventh century CE, Saudi Arabia was divided into tribes. The people were polytheistic. The Prophet Muhammad (PBUH) started preaching that there was only one God and no one else worthy of worship. After initial resistance, people around him began to embrace Islam. After his death, his successors (or caliphs) expanded the Islamic empire beyond Saudi Arabia.

Merchants from Saudi Arabia transported frankincense, myrrh, precious stones, and textiles to different parts of India. In return, they would bring back various spices for their people. These merchants also brought Islamic practices to India.

Mosques were built in the new lands. Cultures mingled and the architecture of the buildings in India had a different, native flavor, not exactly the same as the mosques in Saudi Arabia.

Sher Muhammed was a practicing Sufi. Sufism began early in the history of Islam. All Muslims believe in the same five pillars—declaration of faith (Shahada), daily prayers (Salah), charity (Zakat), fasting (Sawm), and pilgrimage (Hajj). Sufism is not a distinct set of beliefs but more like a mystical way of viewing Islamic teachings. It is seeing connections between the spiritual and the mundane, for example believing that the earth circles the sun the same way that pilgrims circle the Kaaba (the most sacred site in Islam). Sher Muhammed was a thought leader in his Sufi order and had many followers among the people of his generation.

Musahib's family lived in an ancient city called Panipat in the north of India. Over the centuries, three historic battles took place in Panipat. All three resulted when armies clashed from the north and west, trying to expand their reach to the Bay of Bengal. They met resistance from southern forces pushing them north towards Afghanistan and neighboring lands.

Musahib grew up just minutes from the old battlefields. He used to run with his friends through tranquil grass fields, past monuments explaining troop movements. The tomb of the first invading emperor rose only slightly above the ground. The British tried to restore some of the old monuments and install new plaques and guardrails. Children raced up the steps on one side, dashed around the grave, and down the stairs again.

In those days, Panipat was a small city. Sher Muhammed, his wife Fazalunnisa, and their extended families all lived within walking distance. Some owned small pieces of land and farmed for a living, while others had no choice but to work in low-paying jobs.

Musahib's family had no refrigerator, no phone, and no car. These things were not available to the general public at that time. Hardly anyone in the city was privileged enough to own them. On Sher Muhammed's salary as an elementary school teacher, the family barely had money for food, clothing, and domestic articles.

After arriving in India, the British set up operations on the Indian coast. Originally a merchant organization, the East India Company gradually became a potent and influential body with the full support of the colonial government. They brought enslaved people from Africa and harvested their own spices on Indian land, effectively removing the indigenous people from the trade. A series of military strikes eventually brought the entire subcontinent under British rule.

By the time Musahib was born, the people of India were already yearning for freedom. British nationals were in charge of all levels of government, from the crown overseas to the local heads of police and the ministers of the courts of justice. Local leaders often arrived in India fully educated abroad. Even though they did not know much about the local customs and languages, they considered themselves far superior to local people.

Indian citizens were taxed for revenue to support the army, subjugating them to the crown. The wealth gap was immense. British colonialists lived in mansions with native servants to tend to them, while ordinary Indians suffered famine and impoverishment.

Just thinking about all this, young Musahib asked one of his teachers, who was his father's friend, "What is your feeling about this inequity in our country?"

The teacher responded, "It is unfair. I do not like it a bit but I am glad our leaders are working hard to help us all achieve full freedom."

As the conversation proceeded, he asked his teacher another question that was bothering him. "I don't understand why Muslims in India are quite poor and uneducated."

His teacher took a deep breath and then quietly replied, "Years back there was a Muslim rebellion against the British, which was quashed. After this uprising the British targeted Muslims to marginalize them and reduce their power and influence. As a result, Indian Muslims became poorer and the subsequent generations less educated."

As a teen, Musahib often heard his father talk about human dignity and kindness. He was also quite aware of the caste system in Indian society. He thought it was unfair. He wanted to know if Islam encouraged such a system.

When he asked his father about it, Sher Muhammad told his curious son, "No, Islam teaches us we are all equal in the eyes of Allah (God)."

CHAPTER THREE

THE TWINS

F azalunnisa was very young when she got married and became
pregnant. Within a short time, her twins were born and she became
the head of her household. The task was enormous. For a girl who would
still be considered a child, cleaning and cooking while taking care of the
twins was more than she could handle.

After the twins, Fazalunnisa and Sher Muhammed had one daughter and
one son. One additional son died in childhood. The family lived in a small
house in the main city of Panipat, where Fazalunissa was a housewife and
her husband taught elementary school math. Their son Musahib loved
math and because that was his father's specialty, math became a common
language between the two. Young Musahib always wanted to learn new
things and excelled in school.

Fazalunnisa used to wake up for the dawn prayer and spend much of
her time in the kitchen. The family had to be fed in the morning before
work and school. Lunch and dinner required much prep work. Bread was
made fresh every day, kneaded and cooked. Meat had to be cooked with
vegetables almost daily. There was laundry to be done, washed and hung
out to dry. The house had to be cleaned.

Sher Muhammed came home one evening to find his wife scrubbing the floor while the babies cried. She was so busy with other things, she did not notice that the meat in the pot had started burning.

"What is happening?" Sher Muhammed asked, setting his books down on the table.

Fazalunnisa looked up, her eyes full of tears. She raced to the stove, just realizing that dinner was ruined. She desperately churned bits of burnt meat from the inside of the pot. With a feeling of defeat, she removed the pot from the flame.

"The babies are crying," Sher Muhammed said helplessly.

Fazalunnisa lifted baby Misbah and settled down with him in a kitchen chair. Alone in the bed, Misbah's brother continued to wail. Without a word, Fazalunnisa guided one child to her breast, unable to please them both. Trying to juggle all the tasks she was supposed to complete, she felt overwhelmed.

Sher Muhammed picked up the other baby, bouncing him gently. "I think you need help," he said to his wife.

Fazalunnisa looked up at her husband gratefully. For the first time that day, her tired eyes smiled.

For months afterward, Musahib was nursed by his aunt (Sher Muhammed's sister), who had a baby about the same age. Fazalunnnisa grew and matured, and later was able to accomplish all the things she needed to do in a day. By the time the twins were old enough for school, housework was a practiced art. She would make them sit near her in the kitchen while cooking daily meals. This helped her keep an eye on them to ensure they behaved.

Chapter Four

COLLEGE

F ive-year-old Musahib stretched across the kitchen table to grab a mango from a basket in the center. His mother pushed it closer to him, encouraging him to sit down and eat rather than run around the house with the fruit in his hand. Musahib grinned, ignoring her advice. He took a bite and disappeared from the kitchen, leaving his mother to her necessary chores.

Sher Muhammed stood with his back to the door, facing a group of men seated on the floor. Almost all of them had beards. A few wore pants and shirts but the rest were in casual Indian dress. Some were young, others rather old. They all sat silently, gazing up at Sher Muhammed, their faces lit with love and affection.

Musahib threaded around his father's legs, climbing onto a chair to join the class. Sher Muhammed smiled just for his son before returning to his lecture. "I want you to go out to far away villages. You will find people living in those remote areas who do not know how to read the Holy Quran and properly perform their daily prayers. They need your help to learn those important things. Allah will reward you for your sincere work."

Young Musahib's life was a happy one. His parents were poor, but they were well respected in the community. His home was always neat and clean. He studied hard all the way through school, reaching the tenth grade at the top of his class. He held the highest position in the whole district, which consisted of several cities. In those days, tenth grade was as far as indigenous students were expected to go.

"Musahib, let us go for a walk." Sher Muhammed said one day close to graduation.

Musahib put his book down and followed his father through the kitchen to the front door. The late afternoon sun soaked the sky, and children ran down the street chasing each other. Sher Muhammed turned away from town, following the road between loosely packed houses. Musahib hurried to keep up with his father.

"We received your character certificate from school today." Sher Muhammed informed his son.

"Yes, Dad?" Musahib said, curious.

A character certificate was a letter from the school administration designed to help young graduates with their job search. It consisted of descriptions of a young man's study habits, his grades, and an overall judgment of his prospects as an adult. Along with the diploma, this statement about character helped many young people take the next step toward their future.

"You've been recommended as a clerk," Sher Muhammed said, "A good clerk." He smiled.

"Yes, Sir." Musahib nodded. Being recommended as a clerk was among the highest honors a school could bestow on a graduating student. During the British occupation, the goal of the educational system was to produce low-paid workers. Native-born pupils were not encouraged to pursue higher education.

"Your brother is graduating too, but I think he will be happy to be done with school."

Musahib didn't say anything. He kicked a pebble. He had a feeling that he knew what was coming.

"I want to send you to college," Sher Muhammed said.

Musahib held his breath.

"I want to," Sher Muhammed said again, "But...we just don't have the money."

Musahib stopped walking.

"You have to understand," his father began, "I would do anything to be able to help you, but my hands are tied."

Musahib looked away. He found a mango tree in a neighbor's yard to focus on, anything but the pain his father's words were creating.

"You could become a clerk," Sher Muhammed said, "It's good work. Respectable."

Musahib inhaled, fortifying his inner self. "Yes. I can become a clerk." He met his father's gaze again. "Don't worry about me, Father. I am grateful for everything you and Mother have done for me."

Sher Muhammed dropped one hand onto the boy's shoulder. He wasn't fooled. There wasn't anything to be done though, the money simply wasn't there. Without a word, the pair turned and walked back to their home.

It wasn't the end of his dreams, however. After graduation, Musahib made it his business to ask everyone he could think of for help. His auntie came for dinner one evening and while her children raced around the kitchen, Musahib brought up the subject.

"Do you know anyone I could ask for money for my college education?" he asked observing her as she stood arranging fruit on a platter.

His aunt's response was very discouraging, "Why do you want more education?"

"Education is the most important thing one can have to succeed in life," he replied, dodging one of his cousins. "I do not know any other way to come out of poverty. It will also enable me to help my family."

"I'm sorry, Musahib." Auntie clucked, "I don't know anyone with that kind of money."

Musahib questioned the clerk at the post office. The man was always friendly and asked about his family when he went to pick up the mail.

"Do you know anyone who can help me with money for my education?" Musahib asked.

The clerk fit one letter into a box in a honeycomb of compartments on the wall. "Why continue your education?" the clerk asked, "They are looking for clerks. I could put in a good word for you."

Musahib smiled and nodded. "Thank you." He waved at the man before turning his back to walk out the door.

He found his high school math teacher in the classroom over the summer. The hallways were still fresh in his memory as he walked through the front door and past the science hall. As he pulled it open, the door creaked, its wood swollen and hinges rusted. The math teacher sat at his desk, the textbook spread open, copying down an equation.

"Good morning, Sir," he announced himself gently.

"Musahib!" The teacher rose, coming around the desk with open arms.

They hugged briefly before the teacher asked his former student. "What brings you back here?"

"My family doesn't have money for college," Musahib said, forcefully stabbing pride back down. "I was wondering...do you know of any way a poor student might be able to afford college?"

The teacher sighed. He retraced his steps, returning to his seat behind the desk. "I don't know," he said finally. "I will ask around and let you know if I find someone who can help."

"Thank you," Musahib said quickly. He hurried from the building before embarrassment could swallow his determination.

Later that week, word got back to Sher Muhammed that his son was asking everyone for help.

"Son," Sher Muhammed said, folding the prayer rug after finishing the late afternoon prayer.

"Yes, Dad?" Musahib responded

"I heard about a nice place called Malerkotla. It is almost a day away by train. The Raja (chief) of that district is a very kind and generous man."

Musahib waited for his father to continue.

"I was told he has a small residential college that is free."

It was exactly what Musahib had been longing to hear. They purchased a train ticket the next day, and Musahib set out to meet the college administrator. It was a liberal arts college in a town half a day away from what would become the Indian border. The Raja had purchased a small building, hired a few teachers and a housekeeper, and a college was born.

They taught languages, literature, philosophy and math, but none of the hard sciences that excited Musahib. But it was a college, and it was free for the students; there was no tuition fee or room and board. Musahib enrolled and, as he had in high school, graduated at the top of his class.

"Every night, he would read the relevant chapters from his books," Walayet, Musahib's youngest son, recalled. "After leaving the classes he would review those chapters again. He was so particular about everything he did. He would go to bed every night at the same time and be up every day at the same time early in the morning." This unique discipline allowed Musahib to excel in his studies and later in his chosen profession.

The two years of college in the residential school flew by. His teachers and classmates were impressed by his intelligence, hard work and problem-solving ability. But afterward, he faced the same problem he had two years earlier. His family still did not have the funds to support college expenses, and he was still not satisfied with his level of education.

As before, Sher Muhammed came to the rescue. A long time ago, there was a great poet in the city of Panipat. His name was Maulana Altaf Hussain Hali. His most famous poem was an epic describing the ebb and flow of Muslim leadership in the Indian peninsula. Hali advocated for women's education at a time when most people considered it unnecessary and useless.

Hali attended the same mosque as Sher Muhammed; from time to time, they would discuss important issues facing Muslims in India.

One day after the Friday prayer, Sher Muhammed stepped through a doorway into the sun. Behind him, the enclave of the mosque emptied of worshippers. A group of men stood off to one side, under the shade of a big tree. Sher Muhammed joined them, shaking his hand to refuse an offered cigarette.

"There is an Agriculture college in Lyallpur," Hali told them. "I heard students get an excellent education. But I am sorry to tell you there are no Muslims in that college, only Hindus, Sikhs, and perhaps a few Christians."

Several of the men shook their heads.

"That's the way it is," one man said.

"Unfair," the man with the cigarettes said.

"Some Muslims should try to get in there," Hali said.

"What good would it do?" another man argued.

"Agriculture is critical," Hali said. "A young Muslim could bring new technologies to the villagers and help them learn better cultivation methods."

"What did you think of the khutba (sermon)?" Sher Muhammed changed the subject.

"Good," someone else said. "But I don't know why they keep inviting these Imams from other towns to lead the Friday prayers."

Sher Muhammed remembered that long ago conversation about the agriculture college. He started thinking that his son, Musahib, should apply to that institution. Musahib was home after completing his education at the liberal arts school.

"Son," Sher Muhammed said thoughtfully.

"Yes, Dad?" Musahib looked up from the bicycle he was trying to repair.

"I thought about a college for you. It is in Lyallpur. I think you should try to get admission there."

Musahib was listening.

Sher Muhammed continued, "Years back, I once heard Mr. Hali saying that it would be nice if some Muslims studied in that well-known college. I feel you would have an excellent chance of getting accepted. Your mother and I will pray that Allah opens a door of opportunity for you."

After listening to the comforting words, the young man gave his father a big hug and said, "Thanks, Dad. I will ask if they can give me a scholarship when I am there."

Musahib could hardly contain his excitement. His father bought a ticket, and the young scholar was on the next train to Lyallpur.

Chapter Five

LYALLPUR

The British built Lyallpur as a planned city about seventy five miles from the ancient city of Lahore. Though at the time it was part of India, it was deep within what would someday become Pakistan. The city's central feature is a clock tower in the center of a traffic circle. Eight roads emerge from this traffic circle like spokes on a wheel or like the bars on the British flag, the Union Jack.

Photo courtesy of
Google Maps

Each street is a boulevard, heavy with traffic and lit by headlights at night. Cars inch down the road along with hundreds of motorcycles, scooters and

35

bikes. Vendors park on the sides of the road, creating snarls as motorists attempt to circumvent them. After Karachi and Lahore, it is the largest city in Pakistan. Many city residents, either directly or indirectly, are involved in the textile industry. It is not uncommon for Pakistanis to call it the "Manchester of Pakistan." Even when Musahib was a student, Lyallpur was a much bigger, newer city than his ancestral town of Panipat.

Alone in the big city, Musahib stepped off the train with one suitcase in hand. He had an interview with the college admissions officials in two days. He found a hostel and ate the food his mother had packed for him. Later that day, he located the college, called The Punjab Agriculture College and Research Institute, in the city's heart.

For a few minutes, he stood near the college's main entrance and looked at the spiked iron bars resting on hinges. When the time of his appointment drew near, he approached the guards. Once he explained the reason for his visit, one of the guards opened the massive gate and gave him directions.

The administration building was just one of nearly a dozen brick structures within the main campus. The college boasted facilities for studying plant breeding, animal husbandry, agricultural engineering, and food and nutrition sciences. Research departments devoted to cereal crops, cotton, sugarcane, fruits, and vegetables made up the bulk of the school's offerings.

The college's magnificent buildings reminded Musahib of traditional motifs even though they featured modern lecture rooms, laboratories, a museum, and a herbarium. There were several sports grounds as well as a high-class swimming pool, but Musahib already knew all of this because he had done his homework. After spending the previous day in a library, he memorized a series of facts regarding the college and its accomplishments.

He dressed in a British business suit, the only one he had, looking very respectable. Though beards are common in Islamic communities, Musahib was clean-shaven. He left his suitcase in the hostel and arrived at his interview with only a notebook and a pen to demonstrate his scholarly attitude. He found the office of the registrar and checked in with the secretary. A young man, possibly a student, invited Musahib to have a seat.

"Are you a student here?" Musahib asked.

"Yes, I am a student," the young man said.

"What is your favorite subject?"

"Animal husbandry."

"Do you like the school?"

"I am enjoying everything I am learning," the man said with a smile.

"Do you have any tips for me?" Musahib leaned across the desk. "To help in my interview?"

"They always ask for extracurricular activities," The student answered conspiratorially. "Mention if you play any sports or if you have any hobbies like reading poetry books."

Musahib nodded, taking a seat in the waiting area.

"Musahib?" A well dressed gentleman appeared from a white-washed hallway.

Musahib stood, shuffling his notebook to the opposite hand to greet the stranger.

"Follow me, please," the man requested, leading the way down the hall.

Musahib followed closely, entering a big office as the man held the door. Inside, two more men sat at an oversized desk. They stood up to greet Musahib, one extending a hand and the other nodding politely.

"Good morning, gentlemen," Musahib said, deliberately not using the Islamic greeting 'Assalamu Alaikum.' He knew none of them were Muslim.

"Good morning," they all responded with smiles on their faces.

"We are glad you came all the way from Panipat for this interview," a Sikh gentleman said.

Musahib smiled and thanked them for inviting him.

"Please, have a seat," another man requested, rounding the desk to sit behind it.

Musahib chose the only empty seat, a leather cushioned, low-backed chair facing the desk.

"Tell us about your studies," the Sikh gentleman asked.

Musahib opened up about his high school before describing his two years at the small residential college. He told them about his classes and what he had learned, giving his assessment of the curriculum and the teaching materials. He also talked about his study habits and exciting ways he had found to add value to his learning.

"For example," Musahib said, "Simple experiments can be performed using water, salt, and other ordinary things found in most homes." He did not fail to mention that his father was an elementary school teacher. "We both like math and often talk about solving math problems."

At the end of the meeting, all three gentlemen looked relaxed. They congratulated him on his acceptance to the college. "Do you have any questions for us?" one of them asked him.

Musahib drew a breath. "I have to ask for financial assistance."

"Aah." The man sitting behind the desk nodded. "We do have a scholarship."

Musahib felt some tension unwind in his heart.

"But there is only one scholarship," the man continued, crushing Musahib's tender hope. "And there will be many students competing for it."

Musahib held his breath and nodded.

"There is a test in a few weeks. The student who does the best on the test will get the scholarship."

Musahib smiled as he stepped out of the office and said, "I will try my best to win that scholarship."

CHAPTER SIX

THE BEGINNING

Musahib wasn't worried about the test. He had a bigger problem to worry about, and that was how to survive in Lyallpur with hardly any money.

After his interview, he returned to the hostel and finished the leftover food his mother had packed for him.

Dear Father, he wrote, *Exciting news! I have been accepted to Punjab Agriculture College and Research Institute.* He wrote about the scholarship test but did not mention the time he would have to spend in Lyallpur before that crucial test and the beginning of the classes.

Thinking hard about his challenges, he decided to go for a walk. The midday sun baked the streets, bleaching the colors of the hand painted signs and store awnings. Musahib dodged a bicycle, keeping to the right side of the road.

He found a mosque down a side street and ducked inside. A rack for shoes took up one interior wall. He slid his shoes from his feet and placed them delicately into a cubby. The walls were thick plaster, painted green and white. To one side of the foyer, he could see a group of young men gathered in a separate room. They drew water from a well, often a source of communal drinking, available to everyone. He moved past them into the recesses of the mosque. Here he found the prayer room largely empty. He moved instinctively to the front of the cavern and cast his hands up.

"Allah Ho Akbar," he whispered. When he finished his prayer, he had an idea. He had a few weeks before his classes, so he decided to go back to Panipat and try to arrange crucially needed funds.

Liaquat Ali Khan, who would one day become the prime minister of Pakistan, was known to be generous. He and his family had a reputation for helping bright students with their education if their families did not have the necessary funds. Musahib thought someone in that famous family might be interested in helping a young man earn his college degree.

Closely associated with Muhammad Ali Jinnah, Khan was a popular Muslim leader. Like Musahib's family, the other Khan family lived in the Karnal region in India.

Thinking about the generous and caring family, he decided to pay a visit. Dressed in a suit and tie, and armed with a polished resume, he went to call on a benevolent gentleman related to Liaquat Ali Khan.

A driveway curved up from the road, leading to a gate that was unlocked and sitting open on its hinges. Musahib glanced around for a guard he knew would be standing there. He found a man on the left side of the gate and approached him.

"Asalamu aleykum," Musahib said.

The guard nodded.

"I would like to speak with Mr. Khan about a scholarship," he stated the reason for his visit.

The guard held out a hand for paperwork. Musahib waited patiently as the guard assessed the authenticity of his documents. Satisfied, the man passed the papers back and nodded Musahib through. He followed a winding road past flowering trees and lawns manicured to look like British gardens.

A sprawling patio unfolded in front of the house, with umbrellas to ward off the sun and a collection of young people seated underneath. A servant buzzed around the guests, distributing hot tea and collecting empty cups. The servant straightened as Musahib approached.

"Assalamu alaikum (peace be with you)," Musahib greeted the man.

"Wa alaikum assalam (peace be with you too)," the waiter obliged.

"I am here to see Mr. Khan about a scholarship," he said.

The man nodded, almost half bowed over his tray, and disappeared into the house.

"Amazing, what he does," one of the young men present there said from his chair.

"Yes," Musahib said, drifting closer.

Another man leaned across the table, a cup of hot tea in one hand. "Using his Zakat money to send poor students to college. I think it's wonderful."

Musahib halted, staring at the big house with its balconies and wrought iron window frames. Zakat is one of the five pillars of Islam. Every family must donate a portion of their savings to fulfill this religious obligation.

He thought he was there to receive a scholarship based on his excellent school performance. He didn't need charity. He especially didn't want Zakat, which is charity tinged with holiness, God's love meant to support the destitute. His family gave a small amount of Zakat to the local mosque to distribute to the homeless and the beggars. In his mind, thoughts were racing. He said to himself, *"I am not a beggar; I cannot accept Zakat at all."*

He turned around to the astonishment of the people who had gathered at the residence of the wealthy gentleman and walked away.

Unwilling to give up, Musahib discovered another possibility for financial help. A family friend suggested that he should contact Aligarh Muslim University, which Sir Syed Ahmad Khan founded. It was well known that Sir Syed was a great advocate for learning the language of the ruling class. For this advocacy, the crown awarded him the title of "Sir." Perhaps, Musahib thought, he could interest this historic university in the path of a Muslim who had an opportunity to attend a well-known agriculture college in the country.

He was fully aware that the university was far from his native Panipat and could not visit it personally. At that point, he decided to write a letter to the head of Aligarh University for financial aid. The return letter from the Muslim university changed his life forever.

June 14, 1934

Musahib-Ud-Din Khan,

Punjab Agriculture College,

Lyallpur, India.

SALEEM A. KHAN, M.D.

Dear Musahib-Ud-Din,

Peace be with you. We are pleased to inform you that you have been approved for a qarz-e-hasna (interest-free loan) of 50 rupees. The terms of this loan, according to the hadith of the prophet, peace be upon him, do not include any interest. When you are financially stable, please make arrangements to pay the principal in a manner convenient to you. When you pay the loan back, it will undoubtedly help another student in need.

Yours,

Aligarh Muslim University

Musahib was able to use the loan to pay for tuition fees, room and board, and books. It helped him to enroll in the Punjab Agriculture College and study for the scholarship test.

He came out on top when he took the test, as he expected. The single scholarship available to any interested student went to Musahib. He was very thankful to Allah for this blessing. He knew well that he would face many challenges on his future path. At the same time, he was ready to deal with each of them.

Almost sixty years later, his middle son, Saleem, sat down with his father. "How did you take that test?" Saleem asked, "Weren't you nervous?"

"No," Musahib-Ud-Din quickly answered.

"Not even a little bit?" Saleem wondered.

"I always have strong faith in Allah. I also felt confident that my parents were praying for my success. Aligarh University helped me as much as they could in those days. That money was enough for my tuition fee, room and board, and other expenses, only for a couple of months. I knew I could not get more money from any other source. I worked very hard to win that scholarship. It was not easy, but thanks to Allah, I was at the top of the class in that special test."

"But *how* did you know you would get that scholarship?" Saleem asked.

"I needed it. It was that simple," the great gentleman replied.

Saleem responded, "Dad, I admire your faith in Allah and your confidence and courage. Most people faced with such a challenge would just give up. The more I learn about your life, the more I think about writing a book, how you kept succeeding against the odds."

After receiving the scholarship, Musahib felt relieved that he did not have to worry about money. At this point, he started approaching senior students and the staff to learn more about the college. He was impressed when he found out that besides the main college library, there were small libraries for each research section. All these libraries fully supported the students, teachers, and research scientists with the latest literature, journals, and books.

One day he asked one of his teachers about the scope of jobs after graduation. The teacher told him that there were several different opportunities.

"The agriculture graduates work with the government as well as the private sector. Some of them like teaching while others prefer to do research. You may also find them working in agriculture farms specializing in different crops or the food industry."

CHAPTER SEVEN

HARD WORKING STUDENT

Musahib received the largest dorm room as a special prize for winning the scholarship. Lights-out was at 10 p.m. and the school cut the power at that time to make sure no one stayed up past curfew. He used to come out of his room onto the balcony and stand beneath the light of a streetlamp. In this way, he could continue his studies as late as he wished.

He wanted to work hard in those four years to be on top of the class and win the full scholarship every year. He put up with the hardships of weather and mosquitoes for a couple of hours at night to continue his studies. This hard work paid off. He was always on top of the class until he received his Bachelor's degree.

At the culmination of four years, the final test for his Bachelor's degree came full circle to the test that allowed him to win the only scholarship available to his class. He studied diligently for months. Well-known on campus, he saluted many of his friends as he stepped into the test room early in the morning in May of 1938.

The proctor nodded in recognition as Musahib found a seat. Every student received a test book and they were given clear instructions. Musahib answered the questions confidently. When the results came out, he had topped the list. This extraordinary academic achievement earned him the first gold medal of his life.

CHAPTER EIGHT

POPULAR TEACHER

Musahib-Ud-Din accepted a teaching job at the college in the horticulture department as soon as he received his undergraduate degree. In those days, it was unheard of for a Muslim to enter a teaching position at the agriculture college, but he was at the head of his class all four years in a row and the recipient of a gold medal. Considering his extraordinary academic performance, not only was he awarded the position, he became a senior demonstrator right away.

He was 22 when he joined the faculty of the agriculture college. People around him started calling him Musahib Ud-Din. It was no more appropriate for them to use his first name only. Some of them would refer to him as Khan Sahib, which is definitely a respectful way of addressing someone important.

As he had with his studies, he prepared for each class by reviewing his lectures the night before. From the beginning, his students liked him. He asked for their feedback regularly. He would use that feedback to better structure his lectures and make them more attractive. His attention to detail made him clear and easy to understand, an essential quality in a teacher.

One by one his students graduated and started working in educational and research institutions. After several years of experience, some of them were promoted to high government positions as administrators. Several students and researchers trained by him went abroad for higher education (mostly doctorate programs) in the U.S. and Europe.

Quite a few of his students accepted challenging jobs throughout Europe, Middle East and Far East. Because of the extraordinary performance of these young scientists and his own professional publications, he became well known as a superb teacher and a renowned agricultural scientist.

CHAPTER NINE

WORLD WAR II

In September of 1939 when Germany attacked Poland, Great Britain and France declared war. More than two million Indian soldiers fought alongside the British in several different countries around the globe. These soldiers sacrificed much, even their lives, helping Allied forces succeed.

Musahib-Ud-Din, engrossed in his teaching and research, chose not to participate. On the home front, news of the war consumed all talk. Many people had mixed feelings about their loved ones participating in the war. But they realized that under British rule, they had no other choice. People collected food and other necessities to send to the troops. The region of Punjab was heavily involved, sending nearly one million young men into service. Lyallpur was one of Punjab's largest cities, so everyone knew someone who had gone off to fight.

Life went on for the millions of people not involved in combat, just as history played out on the European front. Musahib-Ud-Din grew comfortable in Lyallpur. He had his favorite bookstore, a shop that sold used textbooks and would repurchase books from him at the end of the semester. He often found handwritten notes in the margins helpful. He was frugal; he hardly ever spent money on new books, clothes, or shoes.

CHAPTER TEN

LOVE OF HORTICULTURE

After receiving his Bachelor's degree, Musahib-Ud-Din joined the agriculture college faculty in the horticulture department. On the very first day, the head of the department, Dr. Ball Singh, had a meeting with him.

He told Musahib-Ud-Din about his expectations for the staff. "First of all, I welcome you to our wonderful team. Everyone knows I expect good conduct, respect for other teachers, and excellence in teaching and research. Given your academic record and extraordinary reputation, I am confident you will do well. I know you are interested in research. Just let me know how I can help you."

Musahib-Ud-Din thanked Dr. Ball Singh and said, "I am very interested in the field. I want to learn as much as I can about horticulture. Initially, my research focus will be on mangoes. In the future, I would also like to do research on citrus fruits."

Musahib-Ud-Din often told his students how agriculture was the practice of cultivating field crops and raising livestock. He would share details with them about four main branches of agriculture: crop production, livestock production, agriculture economics, and agriculture engineering. Horticulture, he explained, was the cultivation of garden crops like plants grown for food. He would also tell them about three main categories of horticulture: fruits, vegetables, and flowers.

One day Dr. Ball Singh asked him to give a lecture to his class about types of gardening. As usual, Musahib-Ud-Din prepared his speech quite well. As soon as he started his talk, Professor Ball Singh came to the class and sat at the back. The older professor's presence did not affect the lesson.

As always, with complete confidence, Musahib-Ud-Din began speaking from a position of knowledge. "In our country, there are three types of gardening: home gardening, market gardening, and truck gardening. Home gardening is just what it sounds like, little gardens in patches of land between houses. Over the years, home gardens have provided food for millions of people. Sometimes the owners of these tiny gardens can make a little money by selling what they don't eat. Still, most home gardens hardly sustain a single family."

He asked the class for any questions. Once he had answered their questions, he continued his lecture. "Now I will tell you about market gardening. These are plots of land in and around major cities, not big enough to be called farms but bigger than home gardens. The bulk of vegetables in our kitchens come from market gardening. Very often, sewer water is used to fertilize crops. Even when our college tells the farmers repeatedly that vegetables produced on land fertilized with sewage are a health hazard to humans, they do not seem to care."

He took a pause and asked the students for comments and questions. He listened to them attentively and answered their questions to their satisfaction. After the students had no more comments or questions, he moved on to the final part of his lecture.

"Truck gardening is what many people may visualize as farming. Removed from the city centers, big farmers ship their products by trucks and supply their vegetables and fruits to marketplaces where shopkeepers buy in bulk and in turn sell them to the public."

One more time, he let his students ask questions. He took his time to respond to the students satisfactorily. After the class was over, Professor Ball Singh invited Musahib-Ud-Din to his office.

"Have a seat, young professor," the senior gentleman teased his colleague. "I have heard many good things about you from the students. Today I witnessed what a wonderful teacher you are. I am quite impressed by your confidence, teaching style, and knowledge of the field. I am sure you will be writing professional articles and books one day."

Dr. Ball Singh was right about his assessment of the young scientist. Within a short period of time, Musahib-Ud-Din published research in well-recognized professional journals.

Textbooks in use when he graduated and early in his teaching career were written by British authors. Like other scientists, he was concerned that those books were not relevant to the local environment. Later in his career, Musahib-Ud-Din participated in writing the book, *Horticulture*, which would allow future generations of scientists to better understand the cultivation of garden crops in their native Pakistan.

CHAPTER ELEVEN

MARRIAGE

B efore he even finished college, Musahib-Ud-Din's parents had arranged a match. He had never met the young woman before. They were married in a religious ceremony called *Nikah*.

In those days, rather than an engagement, families preferred to have a Nikah, which according to Islamic guidelines is a legal marriage. That means serious lifelong commitment.

Only close family members attended the Nikah in their hometown of Panipat. Just before the ceremony, two witnesses asked Wazir Begum if she would accept Musahib-Ud-Din as her husband. She said yes and signed a document. Then the Imam recited a few relevant verses from the Holy Quran and asked Musahib-Ud-Din if he would accept Wazir Begum as his wife. After approving the proposal, he signed the same document in the presence of two witnesses and family members. The witnesses signed the official marriage contract which was then registered in the appropriate government office in their town.

This contract clearly specified the amount of Mehar, which was agreed upon by the two families. In Islamic marriage, the groom agrees to give his bride a gift, usually an agreed-upon amount of money. It can also be something material, like clothing, jewelry, or a house. It is called *Mehar*.

When Musahib-Ud-Din and Wazir Begum had their Nikah, he was about eighteen, and she was a young teen. In those days, early marriages were socially acceptable. Female education was relatively uncommon. Parents felt social pressure to secure partners for their daughters while they were young. Social trends have changed gradually over the last few decades. As female education became common, the number of early marriages declined. Arranged marriages are somewhat less common in Pakistan these days too.

Though they came from the same city of Panipat, he had no occasion to venture into his wife's home until another family get-together took place. This event is called *Rukhsati*, a ceremony when the bride leaves her parental home to accompany her husband and start living with him. For Musahib and his wife, there was a period of about four years between their Nikah and Rukhsati before they could live together. These days, very few couples have to endure such a waiting period with no contact options available between each other.

One day, Rasheed Ahmad, Wazir Begum's father, decided to reach out to Musahib's father about the Rukhsati ceremony. Saleem remembers his maternal grandfather, Rasheed Ahmad, as "one of the kindest human beings, a true practicing Muslim and a thorough gentleman. He was also a superb horse rider."

Both fathers were together in the mosque listening to the Imam give the Friday khutba (sermon). Seated on the floor in the prayer room, they nodded appreciatively at salient points in the speech. When the khutba concluded, the men rose to pray, then broke into small groups to talk.

Rasheed Ahmad looped an arm around Sher Muhammed's shoulders, drawing the Sufi away from his flock.

"May I talk to you, Brother?" Rasheed Ahmad asked his friend politely.

"Of course," Sher Muhammed replied.

Together, they found a quiet corner beside a bookshelf.

"How is Musahib doing?" Rasheed Ahmad asked.

"He is doing well," Sher Muhammed replied. "He just finished college."

"And what will he do after college?" Rasheed Ahmad wanted to know.

"Last week he started a teaching job at his college," Sher Muhammed answered, sensing a hint of a deeper purpose.

"Does he have his own place to live?" Rasheed Ahmad asked.

"He was living in the dorms," Sher Muhammed said. "But now he has a little rented house"

Rasheed Ahmad was happy to hear that his son-in-law had a job, and he had a place of his own to live. He looked at his friend and said, "My daughter Wazir Begum is now old enough to be with her husband. What do you think?"

Sher Muhammed nodded and said, "I agree with you. I am going to contact my son." He had not approached Musahib-Ud-Din about that idea yet. Still, he knew that his son was growing up and would be interested in starting a family of his own.

The following day, Sher Muhammed stopped at a local store, borrowing their phone to make a rare call to his son. Musahib-Ud-Din was in his laboratory, reading a chapter on oranges when a servant arrived to tell him he had a phone call. He set his book down, following the man to the phone.

"Assalamu Alaikum."

"Walaikum assalam," his father said.

"Dad!" He immediately recognized the voice.

"I have news for you," Sher Muhammed told his son.

Musahib-Ud-Din waited patiently, eager to share in the excitement.

"Alhamdulillah, you have graduated, just started your first job, and also rented a house for yourself. Your mom and I think it is the right time for you to come home and bring your bride to Lyallpur. We can have a simple Rukhsati."

Musahib-Ud-Din liked the idea. He always loved domestic life. He also thought his parents were right about the timing. He immediately agreed and started planning to visit Panipat, where Wazir Begum was residing.

Neither Wazir Begum nor Fazalunnisa, Musahib-Ud-Din's mother, were given any choices. Their parents arranged their marriages, and they were not allowed to see their husbands before the official Rukhsati. In this waiting time, when the couples were legally married but had never met, it was inappropriate for the young couple to come face to face.

Musahib-Ud-Din caught sight of his bride only once. He was at the Panipat train station, catching a ride back to Lyallpur after school break. He had just washed his hands in the men's room, toweled them off, and stepped out. As he was walking on the platform, he saw a teenage girl sitting close to a woman in a row of chairs facing the train tracks. He thought nothing of it until he passed them, walking towards the ticket window. He glanced over again and recognized his mother-in-law. With a shock, he realized the teenage girl sitting there must be Wazir Begum, his wife.

He dared not approach her, for if she genuinely was Wazir Begum, it would be unthinkable for him to have a conversation with her. A moment later, Rasheed Ahmad appeared from the ticket window, holding up three rail passes. Musahib-Ud-Din recognized the gentleman immediately as his father-in-law. He covered his face with his textbook and hurried away. He never told anybody until after marriage when he was alone with his wife.

"Do you remember that day at the train station in Panipat?" he asked, seated on the porch on a winter day, enjoying the afternoon sun.

She winked at him. "I knew that was you," she said, "I looked at you too."

One day he told his oldest daughter, Naeem, about marriages in the past. She was an adult at that time and newly married. She was surprised to learn how most marriage ceremonies were quite simple then.

After listening to him, she said, "Dad, you know how things are so different these days. Now, wedding celebrations in Pakistan may go on for a week. There is plenty of food: at least one rice and meat dish, kebabs, a couple of vegetable dishes, salads, desserts, and soft drinks. Girls and women sing and dance; sometimes, men join them. It is also common to see women hire experts to paint henna swirls on their hands."

After the Rukhsati, Wazir Begum packed all her belongings and accompanied her husband on a train to Lyallpur. He had transitioned from student to teacher, quickly taking over classes he had once attended.

He was very excited about teaching undergraduate students and having mentors who were always there to guide him.

The young couple's first living space together was a modest townhome on a busy city street. The neighbors, some faculty members, began to notice an unfamiliar young woman in their neighborhood. They started to gossip.

"Did you see a young woman coming and going from Musahib-Ud-Din's house?" one scientist's wife said, a hand propped on her hip.

"Who knows what's going on in his house these days." another woman agreed.

"He should have the decency to be ashamed of himself," the first woman snarled.

Word got back to his direct supervisor, Dr. Ball Singh. One day, he knocked on Musahib-Ud-Din's classroom door between lectures.

"Come to my office," Dr. Singh said.

Musahib-Ud-Din closed his course book and stood, quite alarmed by the tone. He followed his boss down the hall and into his office.

The man closed the door, turning immediately to face Musahib-Ud-Din. "Are you married?" he demanded.

"Yes," Musahib-Ud-Din said.

"Oh." Dr. Ball Singh collapsed a hand against his forehead, grinning in relief. "That's good. You made me worried."

"Why?" Musahib-Ud-Din asked.

"Some faculty members had concerns about a young woman they saw entering your house."

His eyes grew wide, and his thoughts shrunk down to a single emotion: embarrassment. The neighbors thought he was an immoral man, bringing a strange woman to live with him out of wedlock.

Dr. Ball Singh raised both hands to calm his junior colleague down. "Just go to your neighbors' houses with some nice Indian sweets and introduce your wife."

Musahib-Ud-Din shelved his discomfort and went home immediately to tell his wife about his conversation with Dr. Ball Singh.

She looked at him in disbelief. "They thought what?" The stew on the stove boiled up out of the pot. She quickly stirred it with a wooden spoon.

"That..." he searched the ceiling for a delicate way to say it, "They thought...just that we weren't married. They don't know who you are."

"Well," she said, wiping her hands on her apron. "This is my house. I am not just any woman. They need to know I am your wife."

Musahib-Ud-Din was caught off guard. He was still thinking about how to handle the challenging situation, when she made an announcement.

"I'll buy some sweets for our neighbors and tell them who I am," she said, turning back to the stew.

He knew when he had been dismissed. For the rest of the evening, Wazir Begum's mood remained sour. Her husband kept to himself. The next day, Dr. Ball Singh's wife knocked on the door. She brought a servant carrying a big basket of Indian sweets. She asked Wazir Begum and Musahib-Ud-Din to accompany her. Then they went around, distributing sweets as the older woman introduced the newlywed couple to the neighbors.

Chapter Twelve

FIRST MASTER'S DEGREE

It was the year 1941. Musahib-Ud-Din and Wazir Begum had their first child. They were leading happy lives. He was teaching at the college and also doing some research work. Almost three years had passed since he received his undergraduate degree.

He approached Dr. Ball Singh and expressed his desire to work on a Master's degree. The professor supported his idea and told him that he would personally provide supervision. Pretty soon, Musahib-Ud-Din started visiting his department laboratory every day after work.

He would spend a few hours every afternoon in the lab doing his research work, but he did not want to stay too long in the lab because he wanted to be with his family. He came up with an unusual solution. He asked Dr. Ball Singh if he could do some of his research at home at night. The professor knew Musahib-Ud-Din was always busy during the day with his students and could not do his research work with his full attention. He honored the request without any hesitation.

Within a couple of weeks, Musahib-Ud-Din started setting up a small lab at home. The problem was exactly what it had always been: money. A microscope, slides, and other essentials would cost a lot of money, and he didn't have any extra funds. He talked to his wife about this challenge, and they decided to draw upon their small emergency savings.

He was dedicated to his research, staying up late at night examining sections of plants under his microscope. He would slice them as thin as possible with a special razor and put those sections in a petri dish. One at a time, with the help of a tiny brush, he would place them on a glass slide and look at them under the microscope. He had to reject many of them to find the best sections. Once satisfied with his selection, he would record his observations before examining another set of slides. In this way, he would use dozens of glass slides every night.

His son Saleem recalled a moving story from that time. "Mom was always there to help Dad with his work. As he finished each set of slides, she would wash and dry them to be used again. She also used to dab sweat from his forehead with a cloth handkerchief."

"To deal with the hot weather, at times, she used a hand fan because they could not afford an electric one." Saleem became emotional and said, "Dad knew he was a fortunate man to have her in his life. He would praise her at any opportunity. No wonder he dedicated his master's thesis to his wife. The love and affection they had for each other was rare indeed."

As soon as he completed his Master's degree requirements, Musahib-Ud-Din took a required test and submitted his thesis titled, "Bud Formation Differentiation Studies."

His work was reviewed by the assigned academic committee. After a couple of weeks, he met with the committee to defend his research work and answer their questions face to face. A few days later, the head of the faculty informed him that his work was not only accepted, but he had broken the records for highest scores. He went home right away to share the fantastic news with his wife.

"Alhamdulilah," she said. "Thank God your hard work has been rewarded in such a nice way!"

Saleem told an intriguing story about his father's excellent scores. "When he was a full professor, another professor developed an academic rivalry with my dad. The rival professor thought he had found a student who broke my father's academic record."

"Dad told me he became curious. He sent his assistant to the library for the records book. The man returned with a ledger, setting it on the desk. Dad already knew his own score since he memorized it long ago. It was such a monumental achievement that earned him a lot of praise from his teachers and fellow students. When he located the new student's name, he discovered that the student was at the top of the class for that year, but the new score was still four points shy of the record."

"There was another time when a gentleman looked up the score, and Dad was still on top," Saleem said. "Someone may have broken his record since then; after all, no record remains forever."

CHAPTER THIRTEEN

PARTITION

After their first child in May of 1941, Wazir Begum gave birth to five more. The eldest son, Naseem, would eventually become a high school counselor in Maryland. Next came a daughter, Naeem, who would later study botany in her father's footsteps. The third child, Saleem, was born in 1945, a day after the United Nations emerged to maintain international peace and security. He would later practice child/adolescent psychiatry in Delaware.

"My parents used to tease me," Saleem said, "They would say I refused to be born into a world at war."

One day the college asked Musahib-Ud-Din to become the warden of a hostel on the campus. When he accepted this additional responsibility, it came with a free house not far from that hostel. It was an easy walk from that house to the laboratories and classrooms. The family had access to a library, sports ground, and a swimming pool. They had their own front yard and a back yard to grow flowers, vegetables, and fruit plants.

At this point in his life, Musahib-Ud-Din was quite happy with his personal and professional life. But events had hit a breaking point in the rest of the country. People in India wanted total freedom from the British. They wholeheartedly supported the efforts made by their leaders, Mahatma Gandhi and Muhammad Ali Jinnah. Both men were dedicated to overthrowing the colonial government, though they went about it in different ways.

Mahatma Gandhi was a popular Hindu leader. He became famous for non-violent resistance and fasting as a political weapon, fighting hard for Indian independence.

Muhammad Ali Jinnah was the most famous Muslim leader. Like Gandhi, he was also leading the fight for independence. Long before the British exodus from India, Jinnah began to favor a partition. He reasoned that in a unified India, the Muslim minority would be trading one master for another. They lived under the British, and without their own country, he feared they would be crushed under the heel of the Hindus. The plan to divide the newly freed country into two was called *Partition*. In theory, it made sense, but in execution, it became one of the bloodiest events in human history.

Exhausted by two World Wars, the British gave in to the population's cry for freedom. Many political historians believe that the stress of World War II on the British was too much. They felt they could no longer control the subcontinent of India and decided to leave.

They agreed with Jinnah and decided to split India. Pakistan emerged as a new country. There would be East Pakistan and West Pakistan, both Muslim territories. East Pakistan was on one side of India near Myanmar (Burma), while West Pakistan was on the other side near Afghanistan.

Pakistan would now be the area designated for Muslim citizens, and India for the Hindus and Sikhs. Within a short period of time, every Muslim in India would have to migrate to Pakistan, and the entire Hindu and Sikh populations of Pakistan had to relocate to India. It was one of the largest recorded migrations in history.

The problem was that it wasn't peaceful or orderly, but instead, chaotic and violent. Sikhs and Hindus in India attacked Muslims. In Pakistan, Muslims assaulted Hindus and Sikhs. Terrified families rushed to shelters but were rooted out and slaughtered. Houses burned and store windows were shattered. Each minority group fled for their lives, some on oxcarts, some by train, but many on foot. Thousands grew sick or starved to death on the road. According to some historians, an estimated one million people died in the chaos.

Musahib-Ud-Din, Wazir Begum, and their children were Muslim, and the city of Lyallpur (now called Faisalabad) was safely located within Pakistan, but they were concerned about the safety of their families who were still living in their ancestral city of Panipat.

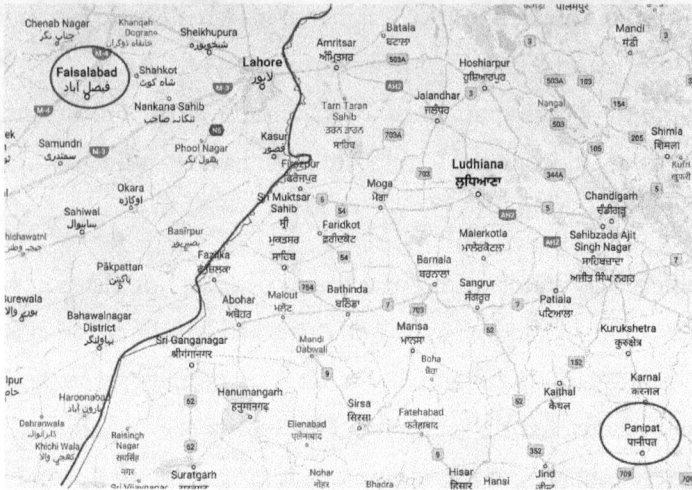

Photo courtesy of Google Maps

Chapter Fourteen

THE TELEGRAM

Musahib-Ud-Din pedaled his bike home from work. He had heard the news on the radio; that the country would split in two. Riots had broken out in Lahore. The city was burning, and there were bodies in the streets. In Lyallpur, there were neighborhoods he didn't want to visit. He told his wife to stay home and keep the kids inside. He could only hold on to hope that there would be peace when the British finally left.

The faculty had gathered in the staff lounge to listen to the news. When the announcement came that the country would divide, teachers looked around nervously. Much of the staff was Hindus and Sikhs. They would no longer be welcome in the college if Lyallpur came out on the Pakistani side of the border. The problem was that no one knew where the border would be. The British wouldn't announce it until the day of separation.

Even without a settled boundary, it was not difficult to speculate that Lyallpur would be within the Muslim-controlled territory, and Panipat would fall to the Hindus. Neither Musahib-Ud-Din nor his parents had telephones. Desperate to get in touch with his mother and father, he ran to a public phone. He tried the corner store where his father often shopped.

"Asalamu aleykum," he said to the proprietor. He.

"Walaikum assalam," the man answered.

"What is the news?" Musahib-Ud-Din did not wait for pleasantries.

"We are leaving," the man said, not asking Musahib-Ud-Din to identify himself or the reason for his phone call. The conversation was very brief. "We are leaving as soon as we can," the man repeated.

"You know my father Sher Muhammed; what about my parents, have they left too?" Musahib-Ud-Din anxiously asked.

"Your father has not come to my store in a few days," the proprietor said.

"Can you please get a message to them?" Musahib-Ud-Din pleaded.

"I think they have already left," the man responded.

Musahib-Ud-Din hung up. He pedaled home as fast as possible to be with his family. His wife was cooking dinner when he arrived. She looked up, and they shared a glance laden with fear. She knew everything; he could see it in her eyes. She had listened to the same broadcast.

He went to her side and quietly asked. "Have you heard from your parents?"

She shook her head, not trusting her voice.

"Me neither," he said.

The children were blissfully unaware of the situation. They kept talking about the toys they were playing with that afternoon. Their parents allowed them to distract from their worries.

"Look at what I drew." Naeem produced a picture of a house with a tree and a family in the garden.

"Very good." Her father kissed her forehead.

Two days later, a mailman knocked on the door early in the morning. Musahib-Ud-Din opened it to discover a telegram from his father. *We are on our way to your home*, it said. Musahib-Ud-Din breathed a sigh of relief. He knew the journey would be arduous, but at least they were safe and on their way. But the reality of the migration would be more brutal than anyone could imagine.

CHAPTER FIFTEEN

BALL SINGH AND LAL SINGH

Professors Ball Singh and Lal Singh were mentors of Musahib-Ud-Din. They helped him with his undergraduate studies. When he joined the faculty, they shared their experiences with him and continued to support his professional endeavors. The senior professors' insights were precious to him, making daily problems easier to manage.

One morning, months before Partition, Musahib-Ud-Din came to Dr. Ball Singh with test papers he was assigned to grade. "Professor?" Musahib-Ud-Din knocked on the door.

"Come in," Ball Singh said.

He entered the room, glancing nervously at the familiar furniture and desk lamp. He had a heavy heart. Something had happened, and as a responsible gentleman and a teacher, he did not want to believe it.

"What is wrong?" Ball Singh gestured to a chair.

Musahib-Ud-Din sat down and produced two identical test papers, each with a different pupil's name.

Professor Singh took them, settling his glasses on the bridge of his nose. After a moment, he looked up. "They were turned in like this?"

Musahib-Ud-Din nodded.

"You have no choice," Dr. Singh said. "You have to report the students to the ethics committee."

"There could be some mistake," Musahib-Ud-Din hesitated.

"That is not for us to decide," Ball Singh said.

"Why would someone do this?" He accepted the test papers back from his mentor.

"College can be a terrifying place." Professor Singh folded his hands, softening his gaze. "Some students may not have the necessary confidence to handle themselves."

Musahib-Ud-Din rose to his feet, still upset. "If I had been a better teacher—"

"You are a great teacher," Ball Singh said. "Everyone says so. I have seen you teaching myself. These pupils, who are involved in cheating, are responsible for their own actions."

After the country split, Musahib-Ud-Din did not see his mentor at work. He had received the telegram from his father a few hours earlier that his family was on the way. He felt somewhat reassured but was afraid for their safety.

"Have you heard from my parents?" Wazir Begum wanted to know.

"No," Musahib-Ud-Din said. "But if my parents are getting out, I'm sure yours are too."

"Insha'Allah (God willing)," she said.

While India had grown toxic for Muslims, the newly created country of Pakistan also became hostile to Hindus and Sikhs. Musahib-Ud-Din had worked closely with Dr. Ball Singh and Professor Lal Singh. He started worrying about their safety.

That same night, when the children were in bed, there was a banging on the door. Musahib-Ud-Din grabbed a cricket bat from the closet and ran to answer. "Get the children," he said.

Wazir Begum hurried to do that, eyes wide with fright.

"Who is there?" he called through the door.

"Professors Ball and Lal." The answer came, and softer, their last names, "Singh."

Like Hindus, Sikhs were no longer welcome in the new country of Pakistan. Afraid that an angry mob might come after them, they fled to their colleague's house. Musahib-Ud-Din was quite aware of the possibility of violence and was thinking about how to help them cross the border unharmed.

He hid the bat, pulled the door open, and ushered his mentors and their families inside. Cautiously, he looked outside and saw the campus was quiet. There was no riot on the college grounds.

"It's safe on the campus, " Musahib-Ud-Din assured his wife.

She appeared in the hallway, recognizing the professors and their families. At her feet, Naeem and Saleem rubbed the sleep from their eyes. "Let's go back to bed," she said quietly.

"Can I offer you some tea?" Musahib-Ud-Din asked his guests.

Dr. Ball Singh set a suitcase down. "I don't think there's time. We've come to ask a favor. A big favor."

"Please tell me, I will do my best," Musahib-Ud-Din said.

When Wazir Begum had finished putting her children to bed, she came into the front room to help the Singh children. She slipped their shoes off one by one and stashed their belongings beside the door. She took them back to the children's rooms and found places for each to lie down. When she was done, Wazir Begum invited the two ladies into her kitchen and put a pot of tea on to boil.

Musahib-Ud-Din was left alone with his mentors.

"We can't take the train." Dr. Ball Singh leaned heavily against the wall.

"There aren't any more tickets," Professor Lal Singh said. "And I heard..."

Dr. Ball Singh flashed his eyes dangerously at his colleague, silencing him. "There aren't any more tickets." There were rumors of massacres on the trains as well as in the neighborhoods.

"You could ride a horse cart. It may take you far enough to catch a bus going towards the border." Musahib-Ud-Din suggested. He offered to help them find a rental horse cart.

"We were hoping you could come with us." Dr. Ball Singh requested of his junior colleague.

"Yes," Musahib-Ud-Din agreed quickly. "I will rent a horse cart. I will do it at first light."

"Thank you." Professor Lal Singh sighed.

"Sit down, please," he requested of his guests. "You have a couple of hours to rest before the morning."

"Musahib-Ud-Din." Professor Ball Singh raised a hand to stop his mentee, "There is something else I have to ask you. We have to leave everything. Will you take care of our furniture and other belongings? Will you keep them just in case we can return?"

Musahib-Ud-Din nodded and assured Professor Ball Singh that he would be happy to honor his request. Then he retreated to the kitchen to fetch tea for them.

Musahib-Ud-Din spent the night in a chair beside the front door. His wife led the two ladies back to the bedroom, where they tried to get some sleep. Professors Ball Singh and Lal Singh sat with Musahib-Ud-Din, occasionally dozing, ironing out business dealings in hushed tones while awake.

"In the top left-hand drawer in my office," Professor Lal Singh said, "There is a grade book. I didn't have a chance to update it. There is a stack of papers that one of my graduate students returned to me."

"I'll get it," Musahib-Ud-Din assured him.

Professor Lal Singh glanced at his friend and junior colleague, "Thank you for agreeing to do this."

He shook his head. "Don't thank me for doing what is right and what should be done."

"I heard stories—" Professor Lal Singh began again.

"Don't," Professor Ball Singh cut him off.

Musahib-Ud-Din rubbed his eyes. "Where will you go?"

"I have some cousins in Gujrat. I am sure they will welcome me with open arms." Professor Lal Singh said, shaking off his fear.

"My siblings and their families are in Delhi. Before I find a teaching job in a college, I will spend some time with them." Dr. Ball Singh said.

"Good." Musahib-Ud-Din nodded. "Glad to know that." Dawn began to break, and the dark beyond the windows faded to gray. Musahib-Ud-Din stretched. "I'm going to rent a horse cart." He glanced at the cricket bat in the corner. "Please do not open the door."

Dr. Ball Singh nodded.

Musahib-Ud-Din walked to the back of the house, to the bedroom he shared with his wife. The Singh women were sound asleep under the bed sheets provided to them. Musahib-Ud-Din gently touched his wife's arm.

She woke up instantly.

"Please provide company to our guests while I go out and rent a horse cart for them," Musahib-Ud-Din whispered.

Wazir Begum nodded, collecting her robe around her.

"If anybody comes to the door, just answer but tell nobody that we have visitors."

Wazir Begum quietly followed her husband to the front of the house, smiling a greeting to the two visiting men. He kissed her forehead before grabbing his jacket and slipping out the door. He hurried to the market. Every additional inch the sun rose into the sky was a minute wasted on their flight. Musahib-Ud-Din found a gentleman with a horse and cart. He asked him to take their little group to the highway leading to the border. The man agreed.

Leading the horse cart back through the college gates, Musahib-Ud-Din recognized every person out walking. He carried himself as he always did, confidently.

As soon as he came home, he hurried inside toward the gentlemen and said, "Let us go."

They woke their children and their wives, put their shoes on, and grabbed their suitcases. Wazir Begum pressed a bag of fruits and a canteen of water for their guests into her husband's hands.

"Don't go outside," he told her. "I'll be back as soon as I can."

"Insha'Allah, (God willing)," his wife whispered, holding back tears.

Musahib-Ud-Din and the two Sikh families hustled out into the dawn, leaving Wazir Begum and her three children behind. The professors helped their wives and children onto the horse cart. They tossed the luggage on board and climbed onto the seat beside the cart's owner. Musahib-Ud-Din took his place among the men as the driver snapped the reins and the horse pulled the cart away.

They drove through the college gates and out into the city. The driver tried to avoid populated areas as much as possible. The professors covered their children with blankets to appear less like a family in flight. As they bumped towards the road, Musahib-Ud-Din grew nervous.

He saw a few men who were out in the early morning. Their horse cart drew a few stares and some pointing and whispering. Any moment, they might be stopped by angry vigilantes bent on revenge. When the city of Lyallpur dwindled behind them and the road promised safety ahead, they began to breathe easier.

Other families were fleeing. They passed several men and women walking and other horse carts full of people. A bus chugged past them early in the morning. The fleeing professors could see haunted faces in the windows.

Eventually, they came upon a traffic jam. A group of men with sticks and knives were searching the carts. Three buggies piled up in the middle of the road; the anxious passengers appeared terrified. A bus was parked to one side, the driver arguing with one knife-wielding man.

A trio of aggressors approached the horse cart, where the professors and their families sat.

"Woah," the first man said, grabbing the horse's reins. "Where are you going, friend?"

They flicked their eyes to the passengers in the cart. "Asalamu aleykum," Musahib-Ud-Din greeted them.

"You're Muslim?" the first man guessed.

Musahib-Ud-Din politely responded, "I am Muslim like you."

"Recite Surah Al-Fatiha," the second man demanded, not believing that Musahib-Ud-Din spoke the truth.

He did not waste time at all, and without a thought, began to recite the first and most well-known Quranic verse.

"Okay," the vigilante cut him off.

"You keep dangerous company," another roughian said. "Where are you headed?"

"I'm just taking them near the border." Musahib-Ud-Din answered.

The first man released the horse's reins. He conferred with his partners, each one of them deciding whether to further disrupt the Singhs' flight. Finally, they agreed to let the small party go. Many other Sikhs did not have a Muslim escort to see them safely to the border. It was that single advantage that may well have saved the professors' lives.

"Avoid Lahore," one of the potential attackers said. "Go in some other direction."

Rolling past the blockade, they tried to avert their eyes from the scene. After a few more miles, they found a bus taking refugees to the Indian border.

"Avoid Lahore," Musahib-Ud-Din told the bus driver.

"I know a way," the driver assured him.

The Singhs climbed out of the horse cart and onto the bus, confident they could make the rest of the journey in peace. Across the border, they could catch other buses to make it to their destination. After a quick but emotional goodbye, Musahib-Ud-Din asked the horse cart driver to take him back home.

CHAPTER SIXTEEN

REFUGEES

Fazalunnisa tried to pack two suitcases. One held clothing, toiletries, family heirlooms, and pictures; the other was full of food.

"No," Sher Muhammed said. "Only one."

Fazalunnisa scrunched up her nose, choosing only a few articles of clothing and a couple of dishes and cups from the kitchen. She crammed them up into one suitcase with the food she had made the night before.

"We have to go." Sher Muhammed approached her, took the suitcase and zipped it shut. He lifted it to test the weight. "This is too heavy." He put it back on the table, opened it, and removed a silver plate.

"No." Fazalunnisa pressed her hands down on top of his, "My uncle gave me this."

Sher Muhammed sighed. He selected some other items she had in the suitcase and removed them, zipping it shut again. Lifting it from the table, he grabbed his coat and hat. The Sufi helped Fazalunnisa wind her shawl around her shoulders and her head. Along with their two younger children, they stepped out of the door of their house for the last time.

They walked familiar streets in the dark, clutching each other's hands. In the distance, they could hear some shouting, but Fazalunnisa couldn't place it. Was it from the farmland to the south or the neighborhoods closer to the city? As they hurried down the road, not needing the light because they knew the way by heart, the shouting grew louder.

When they reached the train station, a crowd was already there. Sher Muhammed pushed his way to the ticket window, past dozens of Muslim families. Men were shouting at the station clerk. Women bundled their children against the predawn chill, steering them clear of the chaos. Fazalunnisa trailed behind her husband into the heart of the mob.

"They are sold out. The tickets are sold out!" The station clerk was shouting.

"I have little children!" one man next to them pleaded.

"Please! My father is old," another man yelled.

"We can't. There is no more space on the train!" The clerk, almost in tears, slammed the window shut.

Sher Muhammed turned to his wife, wrapping a protective arm around her shoulders. Together they pushed their way back out of the station. Outside it was worse. Near the tracks, hundreds of people waited, sitting on suitcases, leaning against each other. After about twenty minutes, a train arrived. On top of the cars, dozens of people sat in the open, trying not to fall off.

People from the station in Panipat tried to board. There was a great rush for the train, but there was no way to get inside. Some people climbed onto the roof to join the masses traveling dangerously. Quite a few individuals were crushed against the side of the locomotive, squirming to get inside but failing because there was absolutely no room.

Fazalunnisa, Sher Muhammed, and their children watched it all in horror. Early dawn light bloomed across the sky, bringing the entire scene into focus.

Sher Muhammed turned around. "Let us walk back," he said.

His wife nodded.

They stepped back into the street, following the road through town. The family fled past the grocery store and the school where Musahib-Ud-Din and his twin brother Misbah-Ud-Din learned to read. They passed the elementary school where Sher Muhammed taught and reached the mosque, the beating heart of their community.

"Brother Sher Muhammed," Rasheed Ahmad called him as he was walking towards him along with his family.

Sher Muhammed looked at his friend sadly. "There is no room on the train."

Rasheed Ahmad smiled, "Don't worry."

He disappeared for a few minutes while Sher Muhammed and Fazalunnisa waited nervously. The road was empty and somehow sinister. The scene at the train station brought the crisis into stark focus. Finally, Rasheed Ahmad returned alongside another man who rode a horse-drawn vehicle.

Fazalunnisa sobbed into her hands, leaning against her husband in relief.

"We are going," Rasheed Ahmad said. "Climb on."

Sher Muhammed handed his suitcase to the wagon driver, who reached down to help them aboard.

Fazalunnisa instantly found Ayesha, Rasheed Ahmad's wife, and dove into her arms. Rasheed Ahmad's two children were with him too. When they saw the children with the other family, they approached them immediately and started talking.

The vehicle's owner kicked the horse gently into motion. The refugees clutched at the railings and each other for balance. They pulled out onto the street to leave the town of Panipat and everything they had ever known behind.

They kept moving along cautiously in the darkness. Other refugees passed them in faster wagons. They drove by hundreds of families on foot. Busses chugged along the road, gaining ground on the horse drawn wagons, and pulling ahead toward safety.

The Khan family was scared, not knowing what could happen. As they pulled into another town, still a long way from the border, it was a huge relief to find a bus heading for Pakistan.

Sher Muhammed helped his wife and children down off the wagon. Along with Rasheed Ahmad and his family, they hurried into the bus station to secure a ride. The bus stood outside the station, surrounded by people begging for a lift. Fazalunnisa clung to her husband as he steered the family out of the station and onto the waiting vehicle.

"Please, help us!" a woman cried, reaching out to grab the driver's hand.

"Can you give us a ride, just to the next town?" a young man was trying to bargain with the bus conductor.

"Only those with tickets," the driver responded, shutting the door. The family thought their troubles had come to an end, but it was not to be. As soon as the bus started, the driver announced, "I cannot go all the way to Pakistan; roads are not safe, and the bus may come under attack."

They felt their hopes diminishing quickly. The driver took them only as far as the next train station. Parking near the tracks, he instructed them all to go inside.

It was a much smaller station than the one in Panipat, and less crowded too. Sher Muhammed hurriedly bought the tickets for both families. They tried to board the first train, and then the second and third, but they were all full. Many passenger trains did not even stop at that tiny train station.

With no other option, they all slept on the roadside for a couple of nights. Fazalunnisa gathered her children, leaning back against the suitcase for support. They ate the food she brought with her but had no clean water to wash it down. All around them, the sounds of desperate people kept them awake.

It was terrifying for the children to be without a roof or a bed. The stories of atrocities were hard to ignore. Everyone they spoke with had some warning about murderous mobs intent on killing Muslim travelers.

After two days, finally, they managed to secure a few seats on a train. Fazalunnisa thanked Allah and started praying for the safety of all her missing relatives. Sher Muhammed thought the worst was behind them and that they would arrive safely in Pakistan within a few hours. But fate had more trials in store.

After less than an hour, the train stopped. Fazalunnisa craned her neck to try to discover the reason. The car was packed with people and there was no way to see outside. Screams erupted from further down the track, spooking the passengers. Sher Muhammed grabbed his wife and children, holding them close as the crowd began to panic.

The side doors burst open and at least seven men with swords and daggers forced their way inside. Without mercy, they slaughtered the people standing near the doors, running them through before turning their weapons on the next frightened passenger. Chaos erupted as the innocent victims tried to flee, pushing further back into the car.

Sher Muhammed grabbed his daughter, shielding her body with his own. Fazalunissa was caught between two other passengers, crushed against a seat, unable to get away.

Allah protected the Khan family that day, because just as death rose to claim them, the train lurched back into motion. The attackers retreated from the train car before the platform sped away, leaving the survivors stunned yet grateful to be alive. Many Muslims died that day, never making it to their destination.

After another few hours spent looking over her shoulder, Fazalunnisa heard someone shouting the word, "Lahore!"

She was the first to scream "Pakistan Zindabad!" which means "Long live Pakistan!"

Reaching the border safely, everyone on the train rejoiced. And yet, their journey was still not over. When the family disembarked, the local authorities took them to a temporary camp with no electricity or clean water. Heavy rains and winds plagued them, drowning their meager possessions and chilling the young children to the bone. They hardly slept that night, praying somehow their son, Musahib-Ud-Din, would find out where they were and come to rescue them.

His twin brother, Misbah-Ud-Din, was also living in Faisalabad and told Musahib-Ud-Din that he would go to the refugee camps to look for their family. Sher Muhammed and Fazalunnisa Begum were clinging to each other, exhausted from their trials. They saw their son in the distance and nearly collapsed with joy.

They ran towards him as soon as they saw him, and everyone started crying. He couldn't know what they had been through, though he could see it had been painful. There were a lot of tears, hugs and kisses.

After this emotional reunion, Misbah-Ud-Din rented a wagon, and they were on their way to Lyallpur. After a few hours, they reached Musahib-Ud-Din's house on the college campus, where he was anxiously waiting for them. One more time, there were tears, hugs and kisses. It was finally over. They made it safely to their destination, unlike so many other poor souls who died along the way.

Chapter Seventeen

IMMIGRANT RELATIVES

After returning successfully from escorting his two mentors to the border, Musahib-Ud-Din was pleased to welcome his and his wife's families into his home. They arrived, luggage in their hands, exhausted but thankful to Allah they were alive.

Musahib-Ud-Din and Wazir Begum moved all the children into their bedroom, giving the children's rooms to their parents and siblings. They were all feeling safe in their new homeland. Naseem, six years old at the time, remembers Partition only as a time when relatives began to collect at his house. Aunts, uncles, and grandparents came one by one until the little government house was filled to the brim. People slept wherever they could, on the couches and the floor.

One day his one aunt arrived with her husband, distraught. She hugged her nephew, kissing him on the forehead. Her husband turned to Musahib-Ud-Din.

"Has Ameena arrived?" He grasped Musahib-Ud-Din's hand and pulled him in for a hug.

Musahib-Ud-Din obliged, waiting to answer until they pulled away. "No. She's not here."

His aunt gasped, turning away and burying her face in her husband's chest.

"We got separated," the man said.

Fazalunnisa, who had herself just made the long and arduous journey, understood. They had slept on the ground beside the road. They passed thousands of people on foot, their eyes vacant and haunted. Ameena, her sister-in-law's child, was somewhere in that mess of humanity or worse. But at that moment, Fazalunnisa didn't want to think about that. She took her sister-in-law by the hand and led her to the kitchen.

Musahib-Ud-Din took his uncle to the porch, where the men shared their stories of how they faced death while trying to escape enemy territories. Out of sight of the women, the man broke down, sobbing into one cupped palm. Naseem, six years old, came around the cluster of uncles and cousins to find his father. Musahib-Ud-Din gently took his son by the hand and led him back into the house.

"Why is he crying?" Naseem asked.

"He had to leave his home," Musahib-Ud-Din answered, not quite a lie.

"Why did everybody have to leave their homes?" Naseem chirped.

"Allah willed it," he replied to his son and brought the child to the kitchen, where the women and the grieving mother gathered around the table. "Go to your mother." He whispered to Naseem.

The child looked up at his father quizzically.

He gave the boy a gentle push.

Instead of going to his mother, Naseem walked forward, putting his hands on his great-aunt's knees. She looked at Naseem through tears. Musahib-Ud-Din could see the final wall in her heart break loose. She hugged little Naseem with gratitude, pulling him up onto her lap.

"Why are you crying?" Naseem touched her hair underneath her headscarf.

"I miss my daughter," the woman sobbed.

Naseem looked back at his father. Musahib-Ud-Din sighed and tried to comfort his aunt. Then he took his son's hand in his, and together they went to the back of the house.

Some of the children staying with them had trouble sleeping. They would wake up in the middle of the night screaming, claiming that people were running after them as they tried to escape buildings. In those days, Pakistani professionals did not have much knowledge of the impact of psychological trauma and how to treat those affected. These children received a lot of emotional support from their families, which seemed to help. Mostly, they could put their negative memories behind them and move on with their lives in their new homeland, where they were all safe.

Chapter Eighteen

RESETTLEMENT

As his little house filled up with relatives, Musahib-Ud-Din began exploring possible homes in the countryside. After work, each day he would ride his bike to adjacent villages and search for modest dwellings. It took months, chipping away at it every afternoon. He returned late in the evening, ate dinner with his extended family, and slept well before the collection of uncles, aunts, and cousins called it quits for the night.

Eventually, he found a community of what could only be called mud houses in a tiny village about an hour's bike ride from Lyallpur. The mud was dried and formed into bricks but was not baked. Each family would have a piece of land to cultivate. He secured a group of modest houses so his extended family could live in their village as neighbors.

He moved his relatives, one nuclear family at a time, into their new dwellings. Uncles and nephews helped move furniture each time, and aunts and nieces cooked bread and curry for everyone. Farewells were said. Household goods were partitioned off. Each house needed pots, pans, and other essentials. Wazir Begum was often taking her children to the market to search out inexpensive items for relatives' homes.

Rasheed Ahmad and his wife and children received one house. They were all going to live there next to other relatives. He had secured a few cots from outside a village store. Together, Musahib-Ud-Din and one of Wazir Begum's brothers walked the cots down the street to the new house, setting them up on the property. Wazir Begum's youngest sister had secluded herself inside the new house, unpacking the pots and pans and trying to find appropriate spots for them. Their father, Rasheed Ahmad, was in the backyard, surveying the land. They were all happy but also nervous living in a new place. It was a village, and they used to live in a city before. They knew it would take them weeks, maybe months, to adjust to life in their new hamlet.

Fazalunnisa packed her suitcase again, the same suitcase they brought from Panipat. This time there was no rush. She filled a bag with clothes, lovingly folded. She found her husband and son in the kitchen, hovering over the teapot.

"Are you ready to go?" Musahib-Ud-Din asked his mother.

"Yes," his mother replied. They would be the recipients of one of the mud houses her son had secured for them. Soon she would have her own home to care for and a piece of agricultural land.

Her heart had grown accustomed to living in this house on the college campus with dozens of other extended family members. She had mixed feelings as she headed to her new residence, leaving her son, his wife and their children behind. Fazalunnisa felt the emptiness but she was ready to move into the little village, where she would be within walking distance of the rest of the family.

They took a horse-drawn vehicle from the city, piled some furniture, clothes, and food onto the cart, and set out across town. Naseem, now seven years old, came with them. The men helped move the furniture into the house: a couple of cots, a small table, two chairs and a trunk to hold their clothes. Fazalunnisa unpacked her cooking utensils and made some tea to drink with the bread from Wazir Begum's kitchen. They sat down together in the cool of the mud house to sip tea and reminisce. When the time came to go, Musahib-Ud-Din took his mother's hands in his own and kissed them.

"This is not goodbye," he said. "You must visit me and my family whenever you want."

"Yes," she promised.

He turned to his father. "Abba," he said.

The two men hugged.

After saying goodbyes, he placed a hand on Naseem's shoulder, leading the boy to the door.

"Wait, Musahib." His mother raised a hand.

He turned back to face her.

"Did I ever tell you about the dream I used to have?" she whispered, tears pricking at the corners of her eyes.

He shook his head, "What dream, Mom?"

"I used to have a dream of two roses," she said. "Of one beautiful and bright red. Your dad showed me your name and your brother's written on the ceiling. That was before you were born, before I knew I would be having twins."

Musahib-Ud-Din inhaled, his breath hot. He placed his mother's head on his chest and wrapped his arms around her shoulders. They stood like that for a long time. When he pulled away, it was with the knowledge that they would share a wonderful life and that she would be safe there.

A week later, Musahib-Ud-Din paid a visit to his extended family. After the visit, as he was working up the energy to bike home, his uncle approached him.

"Thank you for everything you have done and are still doing for the family," his uncle said. "I wonder if you have a moment to talk? I never told you how I escaped."

Musahib-Ud-Din sat back down.

"I could not get on the same train with the family; I had to take another one. They weren't selling tickets anymore, so I just walked onto the next train. There weren't any seats left; it was so crowded, most people were standing." He drew a breath. They could see a group of boys playing cricket in the street two houses down.

"There were children on the train..." He trailed off, watching one boy pitch the ball and a second boy hit it hard with the bat.

Musahib-Ud-Din didn't say anything, just sat with him.

It was a long time before the man continued. "The Sikhs, they jumped on." Another long pause. "With their machetes. They killed everyone. Everyone. We tried to run, but the train was moving. There was nowhere to go, and there were so many people you could hardly breathe. Everyone was screaming and pushing. They were on both sides of the car, coming towards the middle. I..." He took a deep breath and then let it out like smoke from a cigar.

The boys in the street ran forward and backward, between the sticks that served as wickets. The two men watched the game a little longer, long enough for one pair of kids to score two runs.

When the tale picked up again, the older man's voice broke. "I hid under the bodies. I should have fought Musahib. I should have saved the children. I was a coward."

"No." Musahib-Ud-Din reached out and put his hands on his uncle's shoulders. "There was nothing you could have done."

The man put his head down in his hands and wept.

"You're here now. Thank Allah for that, and as always, keep your faith strong," Musahib-Ud-Din said. "You have your younger sister, her husband, and other family members for emotional support. I am glad you are also trying to help them as much as you can. You know better than I that when we help others, Allah helps us more with our problems."

The man sniffed, wiping his eyes clean. "Yes." He nodded, putting the memory away. "Yes, thank you again."

Musahib-Ud-Din stayed there a little longer, comforting his uncle until he was ready to return to the house. It was getting late in the evening and he wanted to be home before dark. He took his bike and left, saving his goodbyes for another time.

Chapter Nineteen

Assistant Professor of Horticulture

At this point in his professional life, Musahib-Ud-Din was an assistant professor of horticulture. The college gave his family a bigger house. They liked this change. It was in a friendly, quiet neighborhood reserved for the families of the senior college faculty.

The children made a lot of friends living there. An expansive sports field was nearby where college athletes often practiced mastering their skills. An experimental fruit garden was only a few minutes away. Musahib-Ud-Din, his students, and junior researchers used this garden to conduct research.

There had never been time off to deal with the trauma of the country splitting. The college remained open, and the staff was expected to continue teaching regardless of their personal issues.

Not only did he fulfill his professional obligations, but Musahib-Ud-Din also spent time working in the community. He devised innovative ways to help people and promoted the programs that earned him the gratitude of his neighbors and friends.

He set up classes for women from the city to learn fruit and vegetable preservation. He taught them how to make pickles, jams, jellies, and concentrated fruit juices. He also helped them learn how to save those products in proper containers. The classes grew quite popular, as they helped many in the community.

Wazir Begum and their daughter, Naeem, also attended the classes a few times for camaraderie and to learn valuable techniques. The knowledge that they had picked up, they shared happily with family and friends. Musahib-Ud-Din often helped his wife pack mangos in salt and vinegar and stacked them in the pantry for his family to use. With growing interest, women's colleges from other cities requested similar courses. Under Musahib-Ud-Din's supervision, more and more young women learned practical food preservation techniques.

Around that time, his son, Saleem, became very ill. Wazir Begum tucked him in and fed him soup and soft food. She sat on the edge of his bed, feeling his forehead. It was scorching. She looked up to see her husband standing in the doorway.

"How is he?" Musahib-Ud-Din asked, coming closer to them.

Wazir Begum shook her head. She gathered the bowl of broth and stood, making room for her husband.

He sat down. His son lay asleep, face pale and sweating. "Oh, Allah," he whispered, "I do not have any wealth. These children are my wealth. The way you listened to the prayer of the Mogul Emperor Baber and saved his son, in the same way, please save my son. You can give his illness to me."

Wazir Begum dropped the soup, watching helplessly as the bowl clattered towards the floor. "No," she said.

Musahib-Ud-Din glanced up at his wife and held out a hand, joining his with hers as she reached across the puddle. He helped her clean up the mess and came back to check on Saleem many times during the night. By the following day, the boy was awake and able to recognize his parents.

"Abba?" Saleem looked at his father fondly.

The professor fell to his knees beside the bed, finding Saleem's hand and pressing it between his own. He bowed his head to the floor, sobs echoing from his gut. "Thank you, Allah," he whispered. Two days later, Saleem was sitting up in bed, demanding reading material. A month later, it was as if he had never been sick.

CHAPTER TWENTY
KINNOW

K innow (or tangerine) is a citrus fruit similar to orange, but it is juicier and has tight skin. It is also known as kinu or kinoo in different parts of the world. Horticulture scientists also call it a high yield mandarin. It is a hybrid of 'king' and 'willow leaf', first developed by Howard B. Frost in Riverside, California.

Kinnow came to the Punjab region of the Indian subcontinent in 1940 from California. The first few plants were received by the department of horticulture at Punjab Agriculture College Lyallpur, where Musahib-Ud-Din was on the faculty.

He was not happy with some of the existing citrus fruits. He was concerned about their taste and the small number of fruits each plant could bear. From the beginning, he took keen interest in the new citrus fruit, kinnow. With his observations over a few years, he came to the conclusion that kinnow would be very successful in Pakistan.

The government was quite interested in the cultivation of Kinnow in the country at commercial scale. But the challenge was how to convince orchard owners and ordinary farmers to try growing a new fruit.

Musahib-UD-Din Khan and scientists working with him frequently visited the big landlords and small farmers, sharing details about Kinnow with them. Gradually they started growing this new imported citrus fruit. They were amazed to notice much higher yield per acre compared to the existing varieties of citrus fruits. They also liked the taste and texture of kinnow. After a few years, kinnows were seen in markets all over the country. Kinnow became a household name. People started growing it even in their home gardens.

Before long, Pakistan was exporting kinnows to other countries. Over the years, Pakistan has exported kinnows to almost forty countries including Russia, Afghanistan, Saudi Arabia and Iran. When kinnow showed up in Iranian markets, people in that country liked it a lot. They named it 'Narangi Pakistan,' which roughly translates to *Pakistan's citrus fruit*. In 1974 when Musahib-Ud-Din visited Iran, he was ecstatic to learn how kinnow was gaining popularity in that country.

Kinnow has undoubtedly played a role in bringing significant amounts of much-needed foreign currency into the country. According to one estimate, kinnow exports were worth more than $200 million in 2021. Some scientists are of the opinion that this amount can be much higher.

In one of his articles, Musahib-Ud-Din wrote that at one point more than half of the area under cultivation for citrus fruits in Pakistan was devoted to kinnow alone. He felt it was like a scientific miracle. He was proud of the fact that the original plants in his experimental fruit garden became the forebearers for millions of others. He would invite his students, friends and family members to look at the site where kinnow plants were grown for the first time.

SALEEM A. KHAN, M.D.

Professor Khan's son Naseem remembers how farmers who grew kinnows were very happy. They could quickly sell their farmland for a premium. Interested individuals were willing to pay five times more to acquire the gardens full of kinnow plants.

After visiting the National Agriculture Research Center in Beltsville Maryland, Musahib-Ud-Din recommended to the secretary of Agriculture Punjab that Pakistan should consider developing seedless kinnows. The secretary took his recommendation seriously and instructed horticulture scientists to work on developing such a variety.

After a few years Pakistani scientists announced the discovery of seedless Kinnows. This discovery helped produce valuable varieties of this fruit at commercial scale. Since then, America and India have also come up with seedless kinnows, which are in high demand particularly in Europe.

Since its introduction in Pakistan, almost eighty years have passed. Many kinnow orchards are quite old at this point. Despite the success of this wonderful fruit, some agricultural scientists in the country are concerned about the future of kinnow. They have observed that in some areas, the fruit is not what it once was. It may not have the same excellent taste or may get certain diseases easily. Scientists in Pakistan have already started addressing those issues and are determined to improve the overall quality.

CHAPTER TWENTY-ONE

KHAN SAHIB'S MANY HATS

The students on the college campus liked their teacher, Musahib-Ud-Din Khan, a lot. Many of them considered him as their mentor and role model. When addressing him, out of love and respect, they would call him Khan Sahib.

The agriculture college had independent departments of horticulture, botany, agriculture, chemistry, sugarcane, vegetables, and entomology. The staff was busy doing research and teaching the students in all those areas.

Once, several heads of departments went out on leave or were sick at the same time. Musahib-Ud-Din accepted temporary responsibilities for a few of these departments. Because he held so many titles, he became a running joke among college students. One day a student asked his friends, "So which new hat is Khan Sahib wearing today?" All of them had a good laugh.

SALEEM A. KHAN, M.D.

Around that time, the college students put on a comedy show, a dramatic interpretation of their lives at the college. They opened the show to entertain faculty, students, and the community around the college. One of the scenes on the show went like this:

INTERIOR - PROFESSOR KHAN'S HOME

HE IS GRADING PAPERS. HIS WIFE STANDS ROCKING THEIR NEWBORN BABY.

Enter three pupils from the left side of the stage.

PUPIL 1

Assalamu alaikum, Khan Sahib, Congratulations on your new arrival!

PUPIL 2

We are all delighted for you, Sir!

PUPIL 3

Well, the little boy is very handsome!

KHAN SAHIB

Why shouldn't he be? He is the son of the head of the department of horticulture, the department of agriculture, the department of sugarcane, and the department of vegetables!

Everyone laughed.

CHAPTER TWENTY-TWO

PERMANENT HOUSE FOR HIS PARENTS

Musahib-Ud-Din was offered the opportunity, as a perk of his position, to buy land very cheaply in Pakistan. It could have been worth a lot of money and represented an estate he might have passed down to his children and grandchildren. He declined the offer, however. "I want my children to achieve success through hard work," he told his son Walayet.

He did not have much money but spent whatever he could to secure housing for his extended family. After Partition, he had moved his parents and aunts and uncles into mud houses in a village not far from the city of Lyallpur. Now, he was afforded an opportunity to find better living situations for them. With their hard work, they had saved some money and were anxious to have something better than before.

One by one, Musahib-Ud-Din guided them to purchase houses made of brick and cement, with good kitchens and proper indoor plumbing.

Whenever he visited his extended family, he would help a new relative pack their bags. They would cross town in wagons, with all their belongings piled on wooden planks. It was a happy move, a step up from where they were before.

Fazalunnisa was not yet that old. She had married young and, within a short time, gave birth to five children. She took medicine for high blood pressure, but her heart was strong. She continued to do all of her housework without any help for the most part. When Musahib-Ud-Din moved his parents to their new home, there were tears. She cried because she had been living in the village within walking distance of her relatives for the past several years. She didn't want something new. But she didn't know how to tell her son, as he had found his parents a house that was close to his college campus residence.

She pulled the remaining shirts off the laundry line, wiping her eyes dry. She found her son and husband in the house, preparing to grab one of the boxes.

"Are you alright, Mother?" Musahib-Ud-Din asked.

She stayed quiet and kept collecting things to put it in boxes.

His father reached down to help.

"No, I can get it, Dad," He protested.

"I am fine." His father waved him off, lifting the box and wandering out the door. Fazalunnisa moved past her son, stepping out the door of her mud house for the last time.

The sun shone directly in her eyes, hanging in mid-air between noon and night. The children playing cricket in the street were older now. One of the neighboring women walked out of her home carrying a bucket. Fazalunnisa waved at her neighbor and continued carrying her laundry basket to the wagon, loading it in the back. Her son emerged from the house, taking the last of the boxes.

Sher Muhammed helped his wife onto the wagon. "Let's go," he said.

The wagon sprang into motion and rocked gently down the road as Fazalunnisa watched her home recede into the distance.

Of all the places that Musahib-Ud-Din and his extended family have visited, from Pakistan to America, the one place no one has ever returned to is India. Panipat, the ancestral city, has been given over to history. Neither Fazalunnisa, Sher Muhammed, nor any of their children or grandchildren ever saw that town again.

CHAPTER TWENTY-THREE

BACK TO SCHOOL

At the same time that he provided food and shelter for nearly all of his relatives, Musahib-Ud-Din was again contemplating his future. He had his Bachelor's degree and one Master's from the agriculture college, but he wanted more. Never in his life had he been satisfied with the level of education he had attained.

In early 1951, he wrote to several prestigious universities. The University of California at Berkeley seemed to have everything he was interested in: a Master's degree program in food science and the prestige of a world-renowned school. With his extraordinary educational achievements and professional experience, he was confident he would receive an excellent scholarship.

He applied to and gained acceptance into the food science department. Now the familiar problem of lack of money reared its head. But it wasn't long before he received a scholarship to attend the school of his choice.

A few months later, he was packing to go to California. His wife sat with him, Saleem on her lap. She was quiet, not discouraging, but sad.

"It won't be long," Musahib-Ud-Din promised, kissing her forehead.

She stayed quiet.

He selected three shirts from the closet and laid them across the bed.

"What's California like?" Saleem wondered.

"I hear it is a very nice place," his father answered.

"When will you be back home?" Saleem asked.

"After two years," he told his son.

"That's a long time," the little boy responded.

Wazir Begum let her breath out in a laugh, loving the child for saying what she couldn't.

Musahib-Ud-Din squinted at both of them. "Not very long; I will try to complete my education as soon as possible and be back home with you."

It was a long journey. At the airport, Musahib-Ud-Din got in line to board the plane to America. Citizens from many nations lined up, businessmen in their suits, a few women in tribal print dresses and college students wearing jeans. There were children and babies among them, older couples with gray hair and glasses. As he waited to board, his ticket in his hand, he could hear announcements in Urdu (Pakistani language) and English.

The passengers got onto the plane. Everything seemed fine during take-off, and there were no issues as the Atlantic Ocean rotated beneath them. The aircraft refueled at a small island off northern Europe. After refueling the take-off was trouble free, but the pilot had some devastating news when they approached their destination.

"Ladies and Gentlemen, this is your captain speaking," the intercom
squawked. "We are having some difficulty with the landing gear. Please
be patient." Everyone who understood English glanced around nervously.
Other travelers didn't have to wait long before the message was translated
into Urdu.

Musahib-Ud-Din leaned back against his chair. The message repeated itself
twice before the intercom fell silent. The beverage carts began working
their way up the aisles a moment later. The flight attendants passed bags of
pretzels to all the passengers and offered sodas to ease their tension.

"I need something stronger than soda." He heard one of the passengers say.

The stewardess looked over her cart to meet the eyes of the other server.
He could see they were scared but keeping a professional demeanor.
She obediently poured the man a beer, handing it over without a word.
Musahib-Ud-Din waited until she wheeled her cart past him.

"Pretzels, sir?" she asked.

"I am praying it's going to be okay," he said.

The stewardess nodded and leaned over to him. She placed a small bag of
pretzels in his hand and kept moving. After another half hour, the beverage
carts came back, and this time they were only selling alcohol.

"What's taking so long?" One woman stood up in her seat, waving an
empty plastic cup.

The stewardess maneuvered in her direction, champagne bottle in hand.

"Have they fixed the landing gear?" A man wanted to know. He held his cup out for the second drink. As the flight attendant tried to reach him, another man begged for more alcohol.

In front of him, an Arab gentleman bent forward in his chair, praying. The babies started to cry. Little children turned to their parents for comfort but found them stressed to the breaking point.

The intercom beeped again; the message in English sent native speakers into a panic. People started shouting, standing, and waving their hands. In tears, women collapsed into their chairs, and men rushed to the beverage carts. The flight attendants tried to calm down the passengers but soon gave up and returned to the back. A few passengers raided the liquor stash, emptying bottles straight down their throats.

Musahib-Ud-Din listened for the message to repeat itself, hardly believing what he had heard. "Ladies and Gentlemen, this is your captain speaking. I regret to inform you that I have been unable to engage the landing gear. We are now circling the runway to deplete our fuel supply. Once the fuel has been depleted, I will attempt a crash landing. For the safety of everyone, passengers and the crew, please remain in your seats with seat belts on." Twenty minutes later, a heart-stopping update came. "Ladies and Gentlemen, we are almost out of fuel. I will attempt to crash land in approximately two minutes."

Musahib-Ud-Din closed his eyes and started soul searching. He had never been a strictly religious person. Yes, he gave zakat to poor people and fasted in the month of Ramadan but did not say his prayers regularly. He was a good man with a good heart. He tried to help others whenever he could. He had always believed that when his time was up, no one would be able to save him. Now, faced with his imminent doom, he silently prayed.

"Please, Allah." He sent his prayer out to the heavens. "I have a wife and five little children. Please, Allah, have mercy." He looked around the cabin at the faces of other passengers traveling with him, yet he somehow felt alone. All of a sudden, hope came back to him. It was as if God had heard his prayer and responded.

Peace. His inner voice seemed to say.

Another message sounded, the voice excited, the words crowded together. A cheer rose, and a dozen drunk passengers tried to come out of their seats. Every man, woman, and child prayed, whatever their religion.

"Ladies and Gentlemen," the pilot said. "The landing gear is now functioning properly. Please remain seated as we prepare for landing."

People wept when the plane touched down the runway unharmed. Strangers flew into each other's arms; women hugged their babies and children. A great cheer rose through the cabin, people shouting and clapping. He found himself crying and wiped the tears away with a shaking finger.

"We did it!" A businessman pulled him out of his seat and into a hug.

He smiled, hugging the man back. "Thank God," he said.

Chapter Twenty-Four

BERKELEY

After the drama of the plane ride, Musahib-Ud-Din didn't like California. To begin with, the English he had learned at home, in college under British occupation, was not the same English they spoke in America. People used words he had never heard of; the cadence was all off. He said things he was sure were correct English phrases, but only a few individuals understood him.

He took all that as a challenge and was determined to change things for the better. He started being very careful about what he said and how he said it. He paid a lot of attention to the nuances of the language, listening to people around him. He felt confident that he could fully understand the textbooks he purchased from the university store.

But he was alone, more alone than he had ever been. He knew no one around him. He missed a house full of family and a neighborhood with many friends.

Berkeley had no halal meat stores then, so he was reduced to a vegetarian diet. Halal means 'permissible,' and when the word is applied to meat, it means that it is from an animal acceptable to the Islamic faith. At meal times, Musahib-Ud-Din missed meat dishes like kebabs and chicken curry. He felt an American salad with iceberg lettuce and chunky tomatoes was like eating wet cardboard.

He phoned the minister (secretary) of education back home in Pakistan. "I feel miserable," he told the gentleman. "I want to come home."

"Don't you quit," the minister replied.

Musahib-Ud-Din sighed. They both knew he wouldn't quit. "I miss my family and friends back home, and there are no halal meat shops here," he complained.

"I understand your challenges. Be patient. I am sure you will soon start adjusting to changes in your environment. Also, you should remember that you are allowed to eat the meat of chicken, sheep, goat, and cow because they have all been declared halal by Allah," he told Musahib-Ud-Din. "Say 'bismillah'(In the name of God) before you eat. And you will be okay."

Musahib-Ud-Din saw a glimmer of hope. Still not fully satisfied, he discussed the issue with a senior student, Ahmad, who was a Muslim from Egypt.

Ahmad responded, "The gentleman is right; the meat of many animals is permissible in Islam." Ahmad also told him, "I go to a farm once a week. They comply with all Islamic guidelines and make the meat as requested. If you want, you can accompany me." After talking to Ahmad, Musahib-Ud-Din started eating chicken and beef almost daily. He decided to stay in California and try to focus on his studies.

He stayed at the international House, which was established on the university campus in 1930 to offer living space for the students who belonged to many different parts of the globe. He liked learning about their customs and traditions. He was especially interested in finding out about the climate and agricultural practices in their home countries. There were many clubs and activities for students to participate in but he kept his involvement to a minimum level and instead spent a lot of time in the library and his lab focusing on his studies and research.

Truman was the president and it was an interesting time on Berkeley campus. It was the Cold War era. The administration banned all socialist and communist speakers. Employees were asked to sign an oath that they did not belong to communist party. Those who refused to sign were fired. Many faculty members were opposed to this idea and started a resistance movement. The university finally decided to rescind the oath. Some people believe that those events paved the way for future campus activities like the free speech movement.

Musahib-Ud-Din worried about his family and how they would survive in his absence. Before he left for America, he asked one of his students to live in the house with his family. This student, Qadeer, became like an older brother to the children and remained a beloved family member forever after.

Thinking about his family, one day he went to see his advisor, Professor Mackinney (with whom he would one day co-publish an article on the properties of grapefruit) just after the start of the first semester.

"I'd like to complete my Master's degree in one year instead of two." Musahib-Ud-Din sat in the red plush chair facing the advisor's desk.

SALEEM A. KHAN, M.D.

Mackinney blinked, then he smiled. "That's never been done."

"Is there any rule against it?" he asked.

"Well, no." The man sputtered, "But you would have to take double the course load."

"I know," Musahib-Ud-Din quickly replied.

The professor emphasized, "I want to make sure you understand that you will have to work very hard."

His immediate response was, "I fully understand, sir."

Mackinney sat upright, studying the young man before him. "Why do you want to complete the Master's program in one year? You have a nice scholarship promised for two academic years."

"I left my family behind," he told his professor. "I'd like to get back to them as soon as possible."

Mackinney sighed, "Okay." He steepled his fingers, "There is a test in biochemistry in two weeks. Show me how you do, then we'll talk."

Musahib-Ud-Din rose to his feet and shook his professor's hand. "Thank you very much, sir," he said as he left the office. It never occurred to him that anything could thwart his plan.

After the test, he met with Professor Mackinney again. The professor was amazed to find Musahib-Ud-Din's extraordinary performance despite all the odds he was facing. Looking at his student's test score, the professor said, "I will make an exception and let you take the course load the way you

116

are asking. I feel confident you can handle it and get your Master's degree before anyone else."

Another problem was money. Always a barrier to his dreams, the financial question loomed. His salary was adequate for all their daily needs, but they hardly had any savings. There was no way Wazir Begum could support the family financially in his absence. The scholarship funds were paid to him directly, as was his salary from the college. He kept his expenses under control and always saved some money. But since the government of Pakistan was relatively new, the procedure for making payments to a family member had not been set up.

Musahib-Ud-Din found a solution with the help of a wealthy businessman in the extended family. As fate would have it, this gentleman was the grandfather of his future daughter-in-law, Saleem's wife. He would send money to this gentleman's business account. The businessman, in turn, would give the money to Wazir Begum regularly. In this way, he was able to support his family from across the oceans. It was a temporary solution until the government caught up with bureaucratic formalities and was able to make payments of his salary directly to his wife.

It was in California that Musahib-Ud-Din continued his pioneering work on citrus fruits. Analyzing ingredients in a grapefruit, he observed the red-orange pigment beta carotene. Initially, he thought he was mistaken. He repeated the tests a few times and then requested his professor to join him. They together performed the tests and had the same results.

Guided by Professor G. Mackinney, Khan Sahib took samples of white, pink and red grapefruits grown in different states, including California, Texas and Arizona. He studied them thoroughly and confirmed the presence of two main pigments (beta carotene and lycopene) in red and pink grapefruits. After this discovery, he published an article in collaboration with Professor G Mackinney, ("Carotenoids In Grapefruit") documenting his research findings in the *Journal of American Society of Plant Physiologists*. This article is still available online today.

We often read how carotenoids (organic pigments like beta carotene and lycopene) are not only responsible for the color of many vegetables and fruits, but they also help decrease inflammation and have cancer-fighting properties

Back home in Lyallpur, young Saleem suffered separation anxiety. He missed his father so much that he refused to go to school. He worried that something terrible might happen to his father in California. Try as she might, Wazir Begum could not force the child to attend school.

Musahib-Ud-Din completed his Master's degree in one year, just as he claimed he could. He returned to Pakistan and rejoined the Punjab Agriculture College with one significant hiccup.

While he was away, the agriculture college gave his job to another man, significantly less qualified than he was. As he had left the position vacant, it allowed the other man to fill in. When he returned from America, he was welcomed back to the college but had to report to a new boss.

"I'm sorry," an old friend said, catching him alone in the staff room.

"For what?" Musahib-Ud-Din set his newspaper down.

"I requested them to save the job for you." The man sat opposite his colleague, "But they wouldn't listen to me at all."

"Things happen." Musahib-Ud-Din shrugged.

"Really?" The man sat back, studying his friend. "I heard you even attended a party thrown by a few individuals to congratulate him for his new position and title. You're not angry with all this?"

"Why should I be angry?" he said. "It is Allah's will. Maybe He has better things waiting for me."

CHAPTER TWENTY-FIVE

SALEEM REFUSES TO GO TO SCHOOL

Musahib-Ud-Din and Wazir Begum had a tearful reunion when he returned from America.

"I am so glad you are back home safe and sound," Wazir Begum cried with delight. "I need your help with Saleem. He missed you so much. He has been refusing to go to school!"

Musahib-Ud-Din was shocked. Education was of paramount importance to him, and the idea that his child might be purposefully neglecting to attend school didn't sit well with him.

"Saleem, come here." He went out to the porch, leaving the door open for his son.

Saleem followed.

"Excuse me, Shamoon." He hailed the old man who cleaned their home and swept their driveway.

Shamoon paused in his work and walked towards the chairs where Musahib-Ud-Din and his son were sitting.

"Shamoon, when you come tomorrow, will you bring my son a small broom and basket? He will help you clean the house and driveway because he does not want to go to school," he said calmly without looking at his son.

Saleem paled. "Abba, Abba." He tugged at his father's shirt. "I will go to school. Please, I don't want to work like Shamoon."

"You must learn a trade if you do not want an education," his father said, winking at Shamoon.

Shamoon smiled back. "Yes, Sir. I will bring your son an extra broom and basket and teach him how to clean around the house."

"No, Abba!" Saleem begged.

"Okay, son." Musahib-Ud-Din nodded his thanks to Shamoon. "Let's go back inside and get ready for school." Within minutes, Saleem was on his way to class.

The school required a test for him to begin again after so many missed days. Saleem surprised everyone when he answered all the questions accurately. Looking at his test performance, the school let him skip kindergarten and move to first grade.

At times Saleem tells his siblings and friends, "After that day, I worked hard and always tried to be at the top of my class."

CHAPTER TWENTY-SIX

HEAD OF THE BOTANY DEPARTMENT

A year after his return from America, Musahib-Ud-Din's youngest child, a boy, was born.

"Dad used to tell me to slow down," Walayet recalled half a century later. "I was always very energetic."

Now there were six children, three boys, and three girls. The children remember their parents going for walks together in the morning and sometimes in the evening. They remember how their father always worked hard to excel and make a positive difference.

"He would come home and bring his files and books with him," Walayet said.

One day, Musahib-Ud-Din found out there was a posting for the position of full professor/head of the botany department. Full professor positions were rare. In each department, a couple of assistant professors were involved in classroom teaching and supervision of research. Demonstrators helped students with the lab work. These supportive positions meant the school didn't need that many professors.

A full professor position would be a significant increase in prestige and salary, but botany was a very different department than horticulture. It was undoubtedly going to be a very challenging situation. Again, Musahib-Ud-Din was confident that he was ready to face all the odds.

He put his resume in for consideration. As was the custom, current faculty automatically received an invitation to interview, so it was no surprise when the secretary called him to make arrangements to be interviewed by the selection board.

He approached the meeting dressed in his best suit and tie, freshly pressed that morning by his loving wife. He pushed the door open gently and stepped into the office. This time, the entire selection board consisted of Muslims.

"Assalamu alaikum," he extended the usual Muslim greetings to the gentlemen about to interview him.

"Walaikum assalam," the committee members replied.

He lowered himself into an available chair, smiling easily.

"So, Musahib-Ud-Din Khan," one man began. "You must understand that you do not have qualifications for this job."

"I believe I am qualified," he responded politely but confidently.

"We have PhDs applying for this position." The man looked at his resume. "You did not study botany beyond undergraduate classes."

"Yes, sir," Musahib-Ud-Din agreed.

"Then why should we consider you as the department head?" the man asked.

"Look at my resume, sir. I feel I can handle this responsibility," he replied.

The committee stared at him.

He folded his hands across his lap, interlocking his fingers tight.

"Well. We will let you know about our decision," one of the committee members said, "Thank you for your time."

"I thank you for this opportunity." Musahib-Ud-Din stood, showing himself out.

Stunned, the selection board sat silently for a moment before the floor erupted into an argument.

"He has more courage than anyone has a right to," one man said, pointing at the door.

"He's conceited," another man spat.

A third man started reading the resume aloud. "Always top of his class from elementary school to college. Two Master's degrees, one of which took him only one year to complete. He studied not only in our college but also at the world-famous University of California at Berkeley. He earned a Bachelor's degree with a gold medal and broke the record in Master's degree. He also won three scholarships. His papers have been published in important journals. Quite a few years working at this institution, always receiving high marks from his students."

The fourth man asked fellow selection board members, "But the question is, can he teach botany?"

After a lengthy discussion, most selection board members were convinced he was the right person for the job. They were impressed not only by his unparalleled academic achievements but also by his confidence and long record of dealing with challenges throughout his life. Finally, they agreed that he would be able to do an excellent job as the head of the botany department. Thus, he was offered the prestigious position on the faculty.

"The next challenge was," Musahib-Ud-Din told his son Saleem forty years later, "Would I be as successful teaching botany as I was previously teaching horticulture?"

The day after officially becoming the head of the department, he went to the library and checked out several books on botany. He read, made notes, and developed lecture plans. The position came with a larger house, greater prestige, and more money. His wife and children were excited to move. Almost all the children would now have their own rooms.

The family stood on the lawn, staring up at the larger structure. They were impressed by what was now going to be their residence, at least for a few years.

"Do you think you can manage such a large house?" Musahib-Ud-Din smiled conspiratorially.

"I'll manage," his wife replied with tears of joy.

CHAPTER TWENTY-SEVEN

CHALLENGES AS A PROFESSOR

After he became a full professor, Musahib-Ud-Din and his family moved into their new, much bigger house. He would wake up early in the morning and go for a walk with his wife. After the stroll, they would have breakfast with their children. Then he would bike across campus to his office.

When the college was in session, he would teach for three hours in the morning and then have a break for lunch, in which he would bike back home and eat with his wife. One more class in the afternoon, and he would be home for the day. Some graduate students would show up in the evening to seek guidance from him about their ongoing projects. His children usually served cold fruit juices to them.

The family ate the evening meal together, and then after finishing their homework, the children went to sleep. Wazir Begum often slept at the same time as the children because she had to be up before the rest of the family to get breakfast started in the mornings. That left her husband alone for an hour or so with the newspaper or whatever studying he wanted to do for the next day's classes. The cycle began the next day again in a comfortable way, like the sun's rising.

Musahib-Ud-Din was now in charge of a laboratory for students, a botanical garden, and a department full of employees with varying educational and social backgrounds. A few of them were with the department for a long time. In contrast, others did not have much experience and needed a lot of guidance to perform their duties well. He dealt with those issues professionally and quickly earned their trust. He was a fair, respectful, and caring boss who expected excellent work and a collegial environment.

One of his main challenges was to study everything quickly and be ready to teach students botany, a subject that he did not have any experience teaching. He was used to taking challenges head-on and facing the odds with confidence. Every day, he read books on this subject. Pretty soon, he felt comfortable that he was ready. Not only did he rise to the challenge of teaching botany, but he became a favorite of students and faculty alike.

After realizing that fodders were needed in large quantities in the country, he became interested in developing a high yield fodder. He worked hard and along with his staff performed many experiments. He tried to cross Napier grass with Bajra (Pearl Millet). The hard work paid off and a new fodder called Bajra Napier Grass (Hybrid) was discovered. One of his students decided to perform research on this fodder for his Master's degree. He requested Professor Khan to provide supervision. He gladly agreed.

As time passed research scientists and farmers started appreciating that this fodder had potential for very high yield and it had many qualities. They also started realizing that it was a very suitable option for certain areas of the country. When newspapers took notice of this new fodder, they interviewed Professor Khan and junior scientists involved in the research with him. Based on what they learnt from them , they published articles.

One day, a junior faculty member, Nasir Ali, came to find him in his office.

"Professor Khan!" Nasir Ali sobbed, slumping into the chair beside the professor's desk.

"What's wrong?" Musahib-Ud-Din instantly looked up from the coursework he was grading.

"My students are making fun of me. I can't teach!" The man fell forward, landing his head on the desk.

Professor Khan stood up, setting his pen down. "Come with me to the class." He gently lifted the man from the desk.

Nasir Ali stood beside the professor.

"Let's go." Musahib-Ud-Din led his junior colleague back to the classroom.

Inside, the students had become a mob, tossing paper airplanes and yelling over one another. Professor Khan let the door clap against the far wall as he flung it open.

"Sit down!" he called.

The students sat. A paper airplane in midair continued its flight toward the window. Most students looked around guiltily.

One of them in the back called out, "We want a day off."

The class laughed.

Professor Khan pointed at that student, "You. Get out."

"What?" He threw his arms open in mock surprise.

"Get out," the professor demanded. "Now. Pick up your books, notepads, and everything else you have."

The rest of the class grabbed their desks and turned their heads away.

The rabble-rouser in the back picked up his books and lurched to his feet. "This isn't fair."

Musahib-Ud-Din held the door as the student walked through, eyes to the floor.

"Where am I supposed to go?"

"You should have thought of that before you were being disrespectful."

The young man's absence created a void in the room, and the silence was thick as fog.

"This is your teacher," Musahib-Ud-Din addressed the rest of the class, pointing to Nasir Ali. "Listen carefully to what he teaches you and show proper respect to him."

"Yes, sir," a few of the students chimed.

The professor stood at the head of the class until the remaining students produced a weak, "Yes, sir."

Musahib-Ud-Din turned to Nasir Ali, placing a hand on his shoulder. "They're all yours."

Nasir Ali never had a problem with his classes again.

CHAPTER TWENTY-EIGHT

INTERNATIONAL STUDENTS

W azir Begum and Musahib-Ud-Din were in the habit of having Eid parties at their home. They invited all the international students from the college on those special occasions. The landscaper would prune the bushes and trim the lawn while the maid cleaned the bathrooms and scrubbed the floors. Wazir Begum spent hours preparing delicious dishes with the help of their family cook.

For Muslims, there are two holidays in the Islamic year. These holidays are both called *Eid*. There is one Eid at the end of Ramadan (the month of fasting), called Eid al-Fitr. This special day is marked by special prayers. People wear nice clothes and cook traditional dishes to enjoy with loved ones. Children anxiously wait for this memorable holiday that always brings gifts for them.

There is another Eid during the month of the Holy Pilgrimage, the Hajj. This is called Eid al-Adha. This Eid is a celebration of the tradition of Prophet Abraham. The legend has it that God commanded him to sacrifice his son. So, the two of them went to a mountain to conduct the sacrifice.

God provided Abraham with a substitute, a sheep to slaughter at the last minute. Muslims the world over celebrate this tradition with special prayers and the distribution of meat from approved animals. According to Islamic guidelines, people keep a portion for their own use, another portion is distributed among family and friends, and the rest of the meat is given to the poor in the community.

The agriculture college attracted students from as far as Syria, Iraq, and Jordan. There were also a few students from Nepal, Thailand, and different parts of Africa. Professor Khan would invite them to celebrate the special events with his family.

To be without your family on Eid would be like being alone on Christmas or any other special holiday. Musahib-Ud-Din was concerned that when everyone else was celebrating, international students would miss their families. He invited them to his home to enjoy traditional dishes and have a good time in a pleasant family environment. All the Khan children loved meeting students from different parts of the world. This experience enabled them to learn about other cultures and traditions.

Professor Khan's students wanted to express their appreciation by bringing gifts for him. Naeem, his eldest daughter, remembered one example where an international student purchased an expensive watch from his country for her father and said, "This is for you, Khan Sahib."

"No, I will not accept it," Musahib-Ud-Din told his student.

"Please, Professor," the pupil said.

"No," the professor shook his head. "It is not appropriate."

"Then I will break the watch," the student responded.

Musahib-Ud-Din simply stared at his student, considering how best to handle the announcement.

The student smiled and said, "Khan Sahib, it is just a small token of my appreciation. You helped me so much. I learned a lot of things under your supervision over the last four years. I have already received my degree. Now I am ready to return to my country and apply all that knowledge and help the farmers learn modern techniques."

At that point, Musahib-Ud-Din reluctantly accepted the gift and thanked the student.

CHAPTER TWENTY-NINE

LIVING IN A MINI MANSION

W hen Musahib-Ud-Din took over as head of the botany department, the house the family received boasted six servant quarters. A cook, a janitor, and a couple of landscapers occupied most of these quarters. There was only one unoccupied quarter. Professor Khan had a kind heart for poor students. He invited two college students to reside there. The students were very thankful as they did not have to worry about their dorm fees anymore and they could easily walk to the college.

His family felt that their new home was like a mini-mansion. Built by ruling Englishmen for their luxurious lifestyles, the house had a big lawn in the front and a smaller one in the back. Originally crops like wheat, corn, and vegetables grew on the surrounding land.

Across from the family's house was a botanical garden, full of many plants and trees. It also had a few rare varieties of foliage from different parts of the world. The college students used to visit the garden and observe what they were learning in their classrooms. Along with Professor Khan, the family often took walks around this beautiful garden. Naeem, the oldest daughter in the family, became so interested in those plants and trees that later on, she studied botany in graduate school.

The children remember the family janitor who had stories to tell them about the Second World War. They would find him sweeping the driveway and circle him.

"Tell us about Burma," they asked.

"Tell us about hiding in the bushes!"

"Tell us about shooting the enemy."

He would often stop working to tell them stories. The children were learning about the war in their schools. One day, Naeem asked him, "Why did the Japanese attack Burma?"

The janitor smiled and explained, "The Japanese first attacked the American fleet at Pearl Harbor. They wanted to eradicate it. But when they could not, they invaded Burma, trying to reach India. We were part of the Indian army under the British, fighting against the Japanese. We were given orders to kill or capture the enemy soldiers."

The children gathered around to hear the janitor tell them exciting tales of how he hid in the bushes, crept up behind the enemy, and shot them.

"Stop telling them these stories," Wazir Begum admonished the man. "You're not getting your work done; instead, you're mesmerizing the children with all this stuff."

Morning walks with his wife were Musahib-Ud-Din's favorite. They would walk and talk about the children. She knew so much more than he did about their friends, school, little colds, and headaches. She would fill him in on the details of the family, and he would often talk about the social politics at work. At times he would share the challenges he was dealing with as the head of a large department. She would listen to him calmly and make a comforting comment every now and then.

They still had their parties, only now, Wazir Begum was in charge of a cooking staff. They invited their close friends and college staff from different departments. They were not keen on opening their home to politicians or bureaucrats. Most people in his position would have jumped at the opportunity to make important connections, but Khan Sahib felt the opposite. He wanted his home to be full of friends and family, not influential people he knew nothing about.

He made sure to invite everyone within his circle. He kept in touch with some of his former students and the faculty at the horticulture department. These colleagues and friends visited him from time to time in his new residence and broke bread with his family.

CHAPTER THIRTY

KIND FATHER

No matter what his position or which foreign dignitary was calling on Pakistan at the moment, Musahib-Ud-Din always made time for his children. Paying full attention to homework was especially important to him. Despite his busy professional life, he always found time to encourage them to learn new things and excel in their classes.

Walayet came to his father one evening, math book in hand. "Abba, show me how to answer this question?" he asked.

His father was at one end of the house. He had a report spread open on the desk in front of him, necessary information for a conference the next day.

"Saleem!" he called for his older son.

Saleem was home from his medical school on a family visit. It took him a minute before he came to the corner of the house where his father was working on his report. "Yes, father?"

"Help your brother," Musahib-Ud-Din commanded, moving a potted plant from the corner of his desk. "Here. You can work here." He set the plant down on the floor.

Saleem came over and took a seat beside the desk. Walayet dropped the book into his brother's lap.

"Which one are you having trouble with?" Saleem asked.

Walayet pointed at the center of the page.

Saleem read the problem. It was related to pre-calculus, asking the students to find intersecting points on a graph. Saleem frowned. He paged through the textbook to try to decipher the equation. "There should be a formula I could just plug the numbers into, and…" he said to his brother as he was getting frustrated. He just couldn't find the formula he was looking for. He returned to the problem and then threw his hands in the air.

Walayet imitated him, mocking him.

"I don't know," Saleem admitted.

Their father looked up. "What do you mean, you don't know?"

"Honestly, I don't know," Saleem said. "I haven't done this for almost eight years. I don't remember."

Musahib-Ud-Din fixed his older son with a stern look. He turned to Walayet and said, "Come here."

The gentleman pushed his work to the side to make space for his youngest child to lay his book down. He read the problem once and explained the solution in easy-to-understand words.

Saleem paid full attention to his father's explanation and stayed to watch Walayet figure out the following equation himself. For his father, it had been almost twenty years since he had encountered high school math, yet it took him no more than a heartbeat to remember.

Wayalet's father continued to support his education through college and graduate school. He was his son's real cheerleader during all the high, low and stressful moments. Wayalet still remembers the time when he had just completed his doctoral thesis in finance; he had made his presentation and handed over three years' worth of work. The first night, he went out for a big dinner celebration with his family. The job was done; now, all he needed to do was wait.

After a month of waiting, Walayet became concerned that he might have done something wrong. Had he turned in the thesis to the wrong office? Had he forgotten to write his name on the cover page? All kinds of atrocities ran through his mind, and he couldn't think logically.

"What if I forgot an important notation?" Walayet complained to his father over the phone. "What if they think there was plagiarism?"

"Slow down," his father said. "Keep yourself calm. Maybe the professor is on vacation. Maybe there are theses from several other students the professor is reviewing before yours. Don't you trust Allah?"

Walayet sighed. "Yes, of course, I trust Allah."

It turned out that the professor *was* on vacation, and shortly after that, Walayet's work was accepted.

"I will buy any books you want in addition to your textbooks," Professor Khan told his children. "But if you lose a book, I will not replace it." Thus, he taught interest in both academics and responsibility.

"He used to tell us to be careful where we put our important things," Saleem remembered. It didn't always go over well with children. Sometimes they thought their father was nagging. If they did lose a book (because eventually, even the most upstanding child makes a mistake), their father would not yell. He would sit the boy or girl down and gently ask them to remember the last time they saw the missing item. With encouragement, the child was usually able to recall and then find what was lost.

The children remember their father nagging about other things, like pouring juice carefully into drinking glasses or putting their socks away. One day Wayalet dropped a cup on the floor and it shattered. As a child, he instantly felt guilty. He should have listened to his father. Didn't his father tell him to be careful? Why had he been so arrogant to assume that he didn't need his father's reminders? But he was amazed that his father did not react in anger.

"Son, things happen," Musahib-Ud-Din said. He put his arm around the boy's shoulders and smiled. "So let's clean this up. I will help you."

Chapter Thirty-One

CORRUPTION

In Pakistan (as is the case everywhere in the world), some influential individuals lacked integrity. Networks of these individuals besieged the infrastructure of the newly formed government. Corruption was becoming common everywhere in the country. Musahib-Ud-Din saw it in the guise of nepotism. The children of the rich and powerful expected to ascend to lucrative careers without having to work for them. Connections were everything, and hard work was not the golden ticket it should have been.

More than once, he felt pressure to hire someone's nephew or son to a post because of family connections. He always declined. His staff earned their positions because of their education and experience, and received promotions due to hard work and professionalism.

One day, he brought his work home with him in the form of two young researchers. They had their tea in the family's drawing room (living room) and were getting ready to move into the dining room for dinner.

One gentleman, we can call him Asghar, was smoking a cigar. He set the blunt down in the ashtray and reached into his lapel. He produced a package, about the size and the shape of a tin of sardines wrapped in brown paper. Then he looked at the professor, setting the container on the table between them.

"What is this?" Musahib-Ud-Din gestured towards the box.

"It's nothing." The man shrugged. "It's just a gift...for your wife." He retrieved the cigar from the ashtray with a wink. "Something she would like a lot."

Musahib-Ud-Din's eyes went from brown to red. He ripped the box from the table, stormed around the other side, and threw the door open. "Out," he demanded.

"But I—" the gentleman gestured at the gift, confused.

"This is a bribe." Musahib-Ud-Din shook the box at him. "I will not have it in my house, and I will not have *you* in my house either. Out now." He stood waiting, breathing fire.

The man narrowed his eyes. Musahib-Ud-Din's reaction had gotten the attention of the entire household. The other guest stood dumbstruck, clutching his hat. Naseem came running. He had never seen his father that angry.

Musahib-Ud-Din crashed through the foyer to the front door, slamming it open. The two gentlemen from the office followed meekly behind him. He took a step back and returned the package to its owner. "Never do this again," he snapped at Asghar.

"I am sorry, Sir, I was just trying to help my brother," Asghar tried to give an excuse for his behavior. He grabbed his hat and left without saying another word. The second gentleman hurried to follow, avoiding Professor Khan's gaze.

Naseem stood just behind his father, stunned, unsure what was happening. Musahib-Ud-Din shut the door and returned to his study.

Naseem followed him and asked, "Dad, what did he want from you?"

"He wanted me to pass his brother, even when he knew well that the boy's performance was abysmal. He wanted to bribe me. I will never do such a thing."

A surge of wealth from young men working abroad flooded quite a few homes in the country. Those already well-to-do spent the extra fortune on politicians and civil servants, ensuring their homes had the best of everything. They bought their children the best schools and jobs, leaving everybody else behind. The system developed into one where it was difficult to get anything significant done without connections or money for bribes. In all this chaos, Musahib-Ud-Din retained his integrity.

One evening, he approached his wife in their bedroom. She was hanging shirts in the closet. He stood next to her, watching her for a minute, long enough for her to know something was wrong. She still said nothing, letting him come to his words in his own time. Finally, he opened up.

"What would you do if we had to run away?"

Wazir Begum smoothed out the collar of one shirt, "Why would we run away?"

"If our lives were in danger."

"Why would our lives be in danger?" She hung the shirt and turned to grab another.

"I'm not...." He searched the floor for the right combination of words. "I cannot play this game of bribery that others do."

She hung the shirt in her hands and turned to face him. "What you are doing is right."

"What if we have to run?" he asked again.

"Then we run," she said.

They stood looking at each other for a long time. She began to hang shirts again.

"That doesn't make you afraid?" He didn't want her to be afraid, just ready in case it became unavoidable.

"No," she said.

"I'm afraid," Musahib-Ud-Din responded.

"I'll pack a bag." She stopped working.

"Thank you." He gave her a big hug.

They did not run. Instead, Musahib-Ud-Din received an offer to join the newly created Agriculture Research Institute, where he became head of the department of fodder (food for livestock) research.

CHAPTER THIRTY-TWO

RESEARCH INSTITUTE

E ventually, the agriculture college became a university. In addition, a new research center was established. They asked all of the existing faculty if they would like to continue at the new university or make a transition to the research institute. Keeping in mind the satisfaction of research over the years, Musahib-Ud-Din opted to move to the research institute.

It was called Ayub Agriculture Research Institute. Initially for about a year he served as fruit specialist and later on as fodder botanist, he became head of the department. In years to come, the institute would develop innovations to help farmers across the country.

Even though they were sister organizations, or perhaps because of it, there was some infighting between the university and Ayub Institute. Musahib-Ud-Din thought it was only natural that the two work together to teach the next generation of scientists while at the same time making breakthroughs. He encouraged the researchers at the agriculture institute and the teaching staff at the university to collaborate. Instead of duplicating research, he requested Ayub Institute to grow their experimental crops and get the university graduate students involved in joint research endeavors.

In those days in Pakistan, the farmers were growing several fodder crops like berseem, barley, sorghum, mustard, millet, and oats. Musahib-Ud-Din wrote a book elaborating on each fodder's growing conditions and explaining the potential diseases and how to combat them. In the book, he emphasized maximizing the yield of different fodders. Over time, along with his staff he performed many experiments and recorded his findings and observations resulting in several quality professional articles.

His former student Habib-Ul-Rehman joined him at the institute. Together they did research on fodders and published their findings In prestigious journals. Habib-Ul-Rehman was very interested in the new fodder, Bajra Napier Grass (hybrid). Supervised by Professor Khan he studied the cytogenetics (how the chromosomes relate to cell behavior) of this fodder, Bajra (Pearl Millet) and Napier Grass. The result was an important research paper, which was published in a well known scientific journal.

Initially Bajra Napier grass (hybrid) was grown by the big landlords and military farms. Professor Khan frequently visited those places to observe the progress . He was very pleased to see the results. He knew that this fodder had many qualities. For the ease of the farmers, he wanted to develop the seeds. But despite all his efforts, he could not. Gradually the small farmers also started cultivating the new fodder and were happy to find out a lot of positive features of it.

As a fodder botanist, Musahib-Ud-Din received yet another home. This time, the family lived in a newly built house in a special section reserved for

145

the officers affiliated with Ayub Institute. Initially, this living arrangement was quite challenging because for several months, electricity was not available, and running water was accessible only for a few hours a day. It was hard, but they learned to live with this reality. Ultimately when the new homes in their neighborhood had functioning utilities, they felt relieved that they no longer had to deal with any of those hardships.

Naseem was then serving in the Pakistan army as a junior officer. Saleem was attending a pre-med program in a boys' college, while the youngest son, Walayet, was in a school for boys. The younger boys rode bikes: Saleem to his college and Walayet to his school. For the first time, the family had a horse-drawn vehicle (called *tanga* in Urdu) with a driver at their disposal. Naeem attended a women's college, while the younger two daughters, Tasneem and Shamim, were still in a school for girls. All three girls and their friends took advantage of this new vehicle to travel back and forth from school.

CHAPTER THIRTY-THREE

PAKISTAN AND INDIA AT WAR

A lmost two months after the British pulled out of the Indian subcontinent, Pakistan and India went to war. It was a conflict over the disputed territory of Kashmir. In haste, a British lawyer, Cyril Radcliffe, drew a line on the map separating the two countries. He did not extend this line into the northern region of Kashmir. About the size of the state of Kansas and populated chiefly with Muslim citizens, Kashmir remains a disputed land to this day.

The fighting lasted until the United Nations intervened, and both countries signed a peace deal known as the Karachi Agreement. This compromise split Kashmir down the middle along what has come to be known as the Line of Control. To this day, the region remains divided into Pakistani-controlled Kashmir and Indian-controlled Kashmir.

After experiencing the trauma and violence related to Partition, ordinary citizens of Pakistan and India had no desire to see a war between neighbors. They were scared but continued their daily activities, hoping the war would stop as soon as possible. Musahib-Ud-Din was busy in his teaching and research work, not thinking much about the conflict.

In 1965, India and Pakistan again had a severe conflict over Kashmir that led to a bloody war. Everyone in Pakistan felt the effects of this war. Combat fighter jets flew through the skies overhead. The Khan children remember how the local government approached every house in Lyallpur and encouraged the residents to dig ditches in their backyards. When there was an attack by air, they had to run to their trenches and stay still until the danger passed.

There was a small airstrip not far from the Khan family home, not large enough to land commercial airplanes but functional for smaller crafts. It was precisely this type of structure that was most vulnerable to enemy attacks. The military protected large commercial airfields, but soldiers could not be spared for tiny landing strips. The unprotected field might be a perfect target for bombing. And if a bomb dropped, it might miss the airstrip and even hit the Khan family home.

It was indeed a stressful time for everyone. For a while, schools and colleges were canceled. Exams were postponed too. International organizations had to intervene to stop the fighting. Both sides suffered losses and many soldiers lost their lives. As a result, the relationship between the two countries worsened.

After the war of 1965, things went back to normal. Naseem and Naeem, the two oldest children, married their respective partners. Musahib-Ud-Din remained busy in his professional activities while the younger four children went to school as usual.

Saleem completed his medical school education and began an internship program at Mayo Hospital in Lahore. In September 1971, he started his first job and moved to Rawalpindi, a big city near Pakistan's capital. In October of the same year, he married and his wife Sabira joined him.

Almost two months after that wedding, India and Pakistan declared war again. The military confrontation ended after only thirteen days but caused extensive damage. For the next several weeks, there were blackouts right after sunset. Trains and buses ran late. Everyone felt scared, not knowing when the enemy planes might attack their towns and villages.

Musahib-Ud-Din and his wife were concerned about the safety and well-being of their three grown-up children and their families living far from them. They tried to stay in touch as much as possible during those uncertain times.

CHAPTER THIRTY-FOUR

RESEARCH INTERESTS

During his professional life, Musahib-Ud-Din was always involved with one research project or the other. In Pakistan when he was working on his Master's degree, he focused his research work on mangoes. The title of his thesis was "Bud Formation Differentiation Studies."

While working in the department of horticulture, at the Agriculture college, Lyallpur he realized that farmers in Pakistan produced tons of mangoes, but often their quality was not as good. He knew that grafting was a better way to achieve superior-quality mangoes. He was happy to learn that some farmers were employing grafting techniques. He worked hard to refine the side grafting technique, which made grafting easier and more effective.

During his stay in the U.S. at the University of Berkeley, when he was working on his second master's degree, his research centered around citrus fruits. He chose "Carotenoids in Certain Citrus Juices" as the title of his thesis. His research findings were published in the *Journal of American Society of Plant Physiologists*.

For several years in Pakistan he was involved in research work on citrus fruits. His observations were published and read by scientists as well as lay people interested in learning about the progress in horticulture in the country. He authored the book, *Our Fruits*, which became quite popular. He was very interested in Pakistani scientists developing seedless kinnows, which were in high demand particularly in Europe.

When he became head of the botany department, he extensively studied medicinal plants and the fodders grown in Pakistan. He supervised the research work of his staff and students. Together they published their findings in well-known professional journals. Professor Musahib-Ud-Din also wrote a book, *Our Fodders*. In this book, he detailed helpful information about fodders grown in the country.

He crossed Napier Grass with Bajra (Pearl Millet) resulting in a new fodder, *Bajra Napier Grass (Hybrid)*. He provided supervision to a master's degree student and a junior scientist, who were interested in doing research

different aspects of this fodder. After their research was over, with the help of Professor Khan they wrote about their findings and got them published.

After working for several years as head of the botany department, he moved to the newly created Ayub Agriculture Research Institute. One of his former students, named Habib-Ur-Rehman, joined him at the new institute. Together they participated in several experiments on crops in the institute's research fields and published their work in prestigious journals..

In 1966 he was promoted to the post of Director Soil Fertility West Pakistan. With this new responsibility, Professor Khan visited many farmlands in different parts of the country. Along with his staff he took samples of various soils, and they performed tests in the lab. He analyzed the yield of common crops using different types of modern fertilizers and it became very clear to him that with proper selection of fertilizers the production of crops could be increased significantly. He also encouraged his staff to develop research projects and provided supervision to them.

Pakistani news media began soliciting his advice. He frequently gave interviews on topics related to agricultural practices in the country. He was also asked to present his recommendations to panels of policymakers. When his expertise attracted the attention of people in power, the next opportunity came his way.

He was asked to head the Pakistan Agriculture Research Council (PARC). In this new position, he oversaw research in agriculture all around the country. He shared the findings of Pakistani researchers with scientists from many different countries at international conferences. He was also delighted to learn about global research in his field.

After visiting other parts of the world, he wrote about what he had learned and personally observed. These writings were beneficial both for agriculture scientists and the general public.

"We are a poor country," he told his son, Saleem.

An adult, and a doctor, Saleem set the newspaper down on the coffee table and listened.

Professor Khan continued, "But no one is starving in Pakistan. There are several countries around the globe where from time to time, the availability of basic food items becomes a major problem. Alhamdulillah (Thank God) Pakistan has been able to feed the masses all this time without much problem."

"Your research and hard work helped improve things in Pakistan ," Saleem said. " You introduced new high yield fodder. Many fruit growers benefited from the grafting technique that you came up with. You also helped kinnow become popular in the country. I know You directed your staff to encourage thousands of farmers to use more appropriate fertilizers ."

He shook his head. "It was always good team work. I am very thankful to Allah. I feel fortunate that I got a chance to work with many brilliant scientists, who contributed to Pakistan's success in agriculture ."

Saleem smiled, "Dad, you are so humble. I am proud of you."

Chapter Thirty-Five

SIMPLE FAMILY LIFE

The family wasn't wealthy, though they lived comfortably in college housing. Musahib-Ud-Din was paid monthly, and every paycheck prompted a family outing to the marketplace. They would rent a horse-drawn cart, and the whole family would climb inside and bump down the road to the inner city.

The marketplace was on an urban boulevard in the heart of the city. Vendors spread their offerings out on walkways, and the family would purchase a month's supply of rice, wheat flour, spices, school supplies, and other necessary items. The children liked that monthly trip and waited anxiously for it.

Musahib-Ud-Din made some extra money by grading papers for various colleges and universities. Some of those institutions were in provinces other than Punjab. They would send test papers in big envelopes by post, and he would grade them following the guidelines they proposed. He mailed them back to the institutions, who would then mail him checks for his work. His extra money helped his family do more things.

"Each time he would get extra money, he would buy Mom another piece of nice jewelry," his daughter Naeem said. Wazir Begum ended up with a small collection. She would show them to her family and friends with pride. She gave away her precious jewelry to her daughters as they married.

PHOTOS

Historical Agriculture College in Lyallpur (now Faisalabad) late 1930s
(photo courtesy of Dr. Tahir Saleem)

Seated: Wazir Begum and Musahib-Ud-Din Khan
Standing (left to right): Sons Walayet, Naseem and Saleem

SALEEM A. KHAN, M.D.

With all his children (left to right): Walayet, Saleem, Naseem,
Musahib-Ud-Din, Naeem, Tasneem, Shamim

SALEEM A. KHAN, M.D.

Musahib-Ud-Din believed that kinnow plants should
be grown extensively in Pakistan
(Photo courtesy of Dr. Naveed Baqir)

Shaking hands with the Governor of Punjab, Amir Muhammed Khan at Ayub Research Institute

(Photo from family album)

SALEEM A. KHAN, M.D.

We are Focused on Agricultural Innovation

Served Ayub Agriculture Research Institute as Fodder Botanist and later as Director General

(photo courtesy of Ayub Agriculture Research Institute)

Meeting with the President of Pakistan, Muhammed Ayub Khan, explaining the progress in agriculture in the country

(photo courtesy of Anwar Ahmad Khan)

SALEEM A. KHAN, M.D.

Served as head of Pakistan Agricultural Research Council from 1974 to 1976

(photo courtesy of Dr. Amna Lateef)

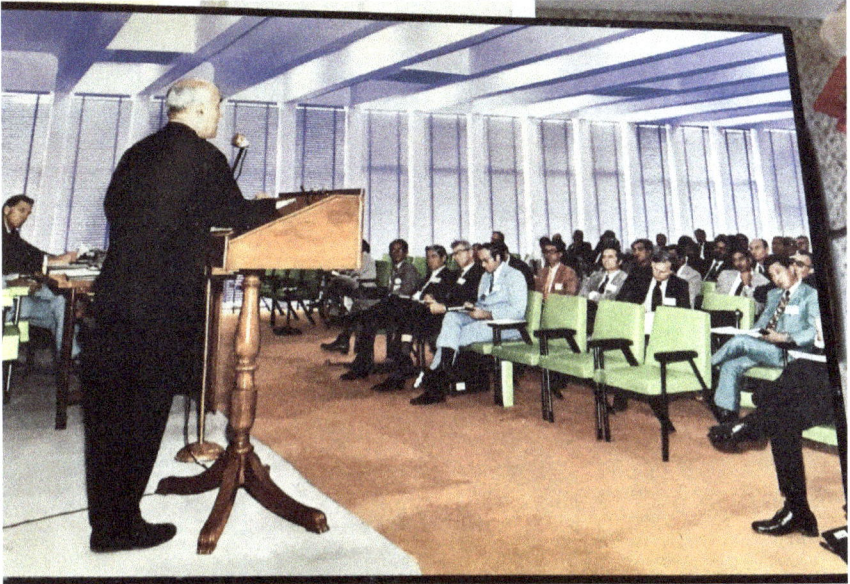

Addressing agriculture scientists in Egypt in 1974,

after inspecting mango trees in the country

(photo from family album)

As Professor Emeritus, taught for many years, at the Agriculture University, Faisalabad

(photo from family album)

Explaining to niece, Raana Sherwani, why some mango fruits fall before they are ripe

Enjoying a birthday party with niece Ghazala and her family

Left to right: Saleem (son), Mona (granddaughter) with her daughter Anisa, Musahib-Ud-Din Khan

A FEW OF THE MANY AWARDS RECEIVED BY MUSAHIB-UD-DIN KHAN

Recognized by Agriculture University
Faisalabad
in 1984 for his extraordinary contributions
(photo courtesy of Tasneem Asmat)

Honored by Agriculture Research Institute
in 2000 for lifetime achievements
(photo courtesy of Tasneem Asmat)

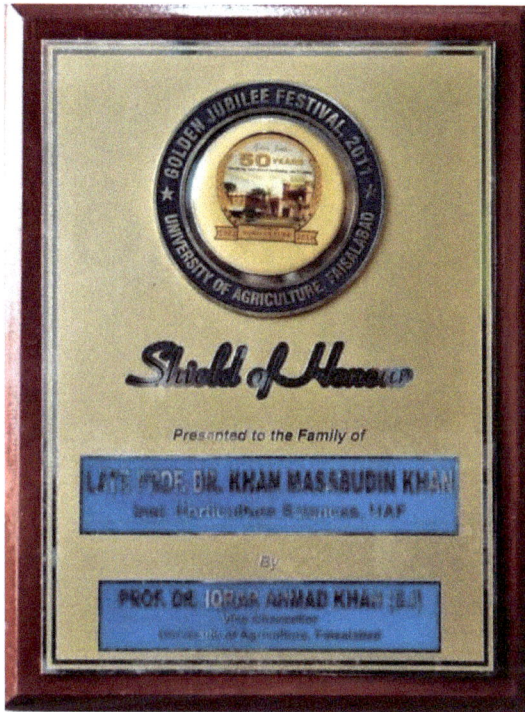

Shield of Honor presented posthumously to his family at the Golden Jubilee Festival of Agriculture University Faisalabad in 2011

(photo courtesy of Tasneem Asmat)

CHAPTER THIRTY-SIX

DIRECTOR SOIL FERTILITY

Almost two decades after the partition, in 1966, Musahib-Ud-Din became Director of Soil Fertility West Pakistan. He was thrilled to have this new position with its challenges and opportunities. Now, he was supervising the work done in soil testing labs all over West Pakistan. His primary focus was helping farmers better understand the need for getting their soils tested. After soil testing, his regional scientists advised the farmers about the use of appropriate modern fertilizers to improve the production of crops.

He believed that it was very important to determine the basic composition of soil in any area. As director, he began with the question, *how best to test the soil?* He reviewed the latest available literature on the subject and helped scientists working under him to benefit from his insight. He would often tell his staff, "Once the soil is tested, you can make appropriate recommendations to the farmers for the most suitable fertilizers."

As Director of Soil Fertility, he became very concerned about several contradictory recommendations that confused the farmers. To combat

174

this misinformation, many field experiments were performed in different parts of West Pakistan. These experiments clarified what was scientifically accurate. He also instructed his research staff to study different combinations of nitrogen and phosphorus fertilizers. He shared the results of these experiments with his scientists and encouraged them to use this knowledge when making recommendations to the farmers.

The family moved from Lyallpur to Lahore, a much bigger and more densely populated city. Lyallpur was quiet compared to the fast paced lifestyle of Lahore. The Khan family was accustomed to living in government housing in the peaceful neighborhood afforded by Ayub Research Institute. It was quite an adjustment for everyone.

In Lahore, Musahib-Ud-Din, his wife, and young children crowded into a smaller house adjacent to his office. He had a government vehicle with a chauffeur at his disposal for the first time. Occasionally, he took a train to his destinations all around West Pakistan.

His eldest son, Naseem, was teaching at an exclusive residential college in town and was living on the campus with his wife and two children. His middle son, Saleem, lived in a medical school dorm. His eldest daughter, Naeem, was married to her father's former student, Anwar and living with him and their children in Peshawar, far from her family of origin. The three younger children remained home, though they were now in college. They used public transportation to get around, as the chauffeur-driven car used by their father was strictly for his official business.

In this new position, Musahib-Ud-Din met many challenges. One by one, he dealt with them patiently and wisely, turning them into opportunities. He worked very hard to establish soil testing labs in as many cities as he could. In his brief autobiography (published in Urdu), he mentioned that at one point almost every district had a lab.

He was asked by the government to represent Pakistan in a conference where many agriculture scientists from other countries were participating. For this international meeting, he wrote a special paper, titled 'Limitations of Fertilizer Use in Pakistan.' In this paper he summarized the work done by his staff and the challenges faced by Pakistan and neighboring countries. Participating delegates were quite impressed by his analysis and insight into the problem.

When he was supervising his professional staff, he discovered a need for a book to help researchers and lab workers improve their work. He wrote this essential text himself instead of asking someone else to do it. It was a manual describing the various soil testing methods relevant to Pakistan. This book was available for many years on Amazon.

CHAPTER THIRTY-SEVEN

EAST PAKISTAN AND WEST PAKISTAN

P akistan began as a Muslim-majority country, carved out from India as a place where Muslims could determine their own fate. Initially, the country consisted of two parts: East Pakistan and West Pakistan. These two parts were separated by India and lay more than a thousand miles apart. The primary language spoken in West Pakistan was Urdu, while people in East Pakistan spoke Bengali.

East Pakistan produced more marketable goods than West Pakistan. Their primary export was jute, a reed which has multiple uses including cloth manufacturing. East Pakistan was more densely populated than West Pakistan, even though the west was a much more extensive area.

Muhammad Ali Jinnah, Governor-General of Pakistan, declared that Urdu would be the official language of both parts of Pakistan. This declaration came as an insult to East Pakistan. People who spoke Bengali complained that Mr. Jinnah did not care about them and their language. Issues related to Kashmir, the wars with India, and the question of equal rights for East Pakistan caused increasing political unrest.

The government of Pakistan made serious efforts to keep the two very different parts of the country together. An artists' exchange program sent artists from East Pakistan to West Pakistan and from west to east. The government created special scholarships to encourage students of professional schools to study in East Pakistan from West Pakistan and vice versa. School aged children from East Pakistan made brief visits to West Pakistan at the government's expense. The Khan children were very excited to meet those students and they even tried to learn a few words of the Bengali language from them.

In 1969, President Ayub Khan stepped down, and General Yahya Khan, commander-in-chief of the military, took over. In 1971, elections brought Sheikh Mujibur Rahman to power in East Pakistan. While his party won a majority of the seats in the National Assembly, the people of East Pakistan were still unhappy. They felt strongly that they were not given equal rights. They wanted a separate country of their own. Incidents of violence increased, prompting East Pakistan to take up arms. India joined the military conflict, and together with the newly formed Bangladesh, they defeated West Pakistan in less than two weeks.

In 1971, when East Pakistan declared its independence and became Bangladesh, some Bengali professionals had federal government jobs in West Pakistan. They remembered the violence and bloodshed during the partition of Pakistan and India in 1947. No wonder they were scared that history might repeat itself! Musahib-Ud-Din was very concerned about those professionals and this situation reminded him of how he had to help his mentors Dr. Ball Singh and Lal Singh escape before.

A Bengali agriculture scientist, Dr. Kamal, lived in Naeem's neighborhood. Musahib-Ud-Din would visit him every time he was in Peshawar with his daughter and her family. Over a period of several years, Musahib-Ud-Din and Dr. Kamal became good friends. They would often discuss challenges the country was facing to feed the growing population.

In 1971, after Bangladesh won its independence, Dr. Kamal and his family suddenly disappeared. Naeem mentioned it in a phone call to her father.

"You remember Dr. Kamal?" she asked hesitantly.

"Of course," her father said.

"I haven't seen him, his wife or children in a few days." Naeem struggled to put her fear into words. "I went around to their house to knock on their door, but no one answered. None of the neighbors have seen them either."

A few weeks later, Naeem received a letter. With shaking hands, she opened the envelope, reading the missive from top to bottom before finally releasing her breath.

Assalamu alaikum,

I apologize for leaving without saying goodbye. The situation in the country made time a precious commodity. Before the sunrise almost a month ago, we packed a few possessions and left our home. I had a connection that offered to take us over the border into Afghanistan on camelback. We were able to avoid detection and arrived safely in our neighboring country. From there, we traveled to our new homeland of Bangladesh, where we have found a house, Alhamdulillah, and are living well.

Now that our journey is over, I wanted to take the time to let you and your father know that your friendship has always been appreciated. May Allah reward you with goodness.

Dr. Kamal

CHAPTER THIRTY-EIGHT

MEETING PRESIDENT AYUB KHAN

Pakistan experienced many changes in government in the early years. Muhammad Ali Jinnah became the first Governor General of Pakistan. In 1956, the first constitution was approved, making Iskander Mirza Pakistan's first president. Ayub Khan became Chief Martial Law Administrator two years later when the constitution was repealed. On the orders of Ayub Khan, President Mirza was arrested and exiled. Ayub Khan installed himself as the President, assuming all the powers of the office immediately.

Musahib-Ud-Din witnessed these twists and turns in the history of his beloved country and like millions of other Pakistanis, prayed for stability. Though he was unelected, people soon appreciated how the new President was governing. The country became stable and established a good name on the international stage.

SALEEM A. KHAN, M.D.

In 1963, Ayub Khan visited the U.S. to meet President Kennedy. In front of thousands of Americans, both presidents rode in a motorcade across Washington D.C. and shared dinner. This well-publicized visit helped increase Ayub Khan's popularity both at home and abroad.

Professor Musahib-Ud-Din met President Ayub Khan at a fruit and vegetable exhibition. He knew that Ayub Khan had studied at the famous Aligarh Muslim University and was also a graduate of the British Royal Military College at Sandhurst. Professor Khan told his staff that he had a lot of respect for the President.

The event in question was a big deal. It was meant to educate the public and policy makers about the agricultural achievements of farmers far and wide. Musahib-Ud-Din was involved in overseeing the entire affair, ensuring all the exhibitors arrived and set up their stations. He made sure the invitees found their way around the venue and that security was in place. He was unaware that the President would attend until the day of the exhibition.

Professor Khan stood beside one of the exhibitors, a man displaying barrels of kinnows. They discussed that year's yield and the expected price of the fruit in foreign markets.

"Sir," A young clerk hustled up to them. "We've just been informed that President Ayub Khan will be here shortly."

Musahib-Ud-Din set the kinnow from his hand back into its barrel. The fruit vendor gaped, inhaled, and appeared nervous. He had never seen the President of Pakistan.

"Alert security," Professor Musahib-Ud-Din said. "Make sure the custodial staff keep the venue in the best shape and let me know when they arrive."

"Yes, Sir." The clerk darted away through the crowd.

Musahib-Ud-Din turned to walk away down the aisle of tables, scanning each display. He selected representative samples of fruits and vegetables, most from well-known farms and some from the fields of small farmers too. He chose various planting techniques, including grafting and seed planting. He also selected a few samples of crops that were bringing value to the market and showed promise for years to come.

"Sir." The clerk found him again in front of a display of maize plants. "The President is here."

Musahib-Ud-Din followed the young man to the front of the venue. Ayub Khan stood just inside the door, surrounded by his entourage: a dozen men in plain clothes and a few in business attire. The President was about six feet two inches tall with thinning hair and an easy smile. For this occasion, he had rejected his military uniform and dressed instead in a gray suit with a red tie.

"Asalamu alaikum Mr. President." Musahib-Ud-Din offered a hand.

"Mr. Khan." The President indicated that he knew Musahib-Ud-Din's name.

"May I show you around?" Professor Khan gestured towards the exhibition.

President Khan nodded in approval, and with his bodyguards trailing, they visited all the stations the host committee had already chosen for the President.

"This is the kinnow." They stopped at the kinnow display. Musahib-Ud-Din chose several ripe fruits to place in a bag, which he would later offer to the President's staff. "It is doing well on the global market." From one side, a photographer wanted to take a few pictures. The President nodded his approval.

"Try this, Sir," Musahib-Ud-Din stopped at a juice stall, offering a glass of freshly squeezed grapefruit juice to the President.

Without any hesitation, President Ayub Khan took a sip. "Delicious," he said and started to drink again.

A nervous staff member came up behind the President and gently removed the glass from his hand.

At the end of the tour, as Musahib-Ud-Din presented Ayub Khan with a selection of fruits and vegetables, the President thanked him for his work. The President voiced admiration for Khan Sahib and other hard-working agriculture scientists, whose efforts made it possible to support the growing population of Pakistan.

After the event, Musahib-Ud-Din went back to his office. He hardly sat down in his chair when the President's special security police barged in without knocking.

"Why did you offer the President a glass of juice?" one man asked.

"Who is the owner of that stall?" Another man pounded his palms against the desk.

"What was in the juice?" a third man yelled, arms crossed.

Musahib-Ud-Din wasn't sure whom to answer first. "It was from a nearby orchard, and the gentleman owner of the orchard pressed a grapefruit to demonstrate its nice taste."

"The President cannot be offered food or drinks without our full knowledge of their origins and security clearance. We would like to take a few samples of that juice," one of the security guards demanded.

Professor Khan rose from his seat, and accompanied the three security officers back to the exhibition hall. They found the grapefruit stand and secured a few samples of the juice. After asking many questions of the stand owner and a few other individuals, they decided that Musahib-Ud-Din did not have any malicious intentions. They let him go but warned him to be very careful in the future.

"I should have known better," he told his daughter, Naeem, many years later. "You cannot offer anything to the President to eat or drink without clearing it with the special staff."

Chapter Thirty-Nine

PAKISTAN AGRICULTURE RESEARCH COUNCIL (PARC)

M usahib-Ud-Din worked tirelessly up the ladder until he became head of the Pakistan Agriculture Research Council (PARC). PARC was a high-level government assignment for very experienced individuals with impressive academic backgrounds. In this new prestigious position, he oversaw agriculture research in every region. There were ongoing projects dealing with fruits, vegetables and different kinds of grains. The research council was interested in advancing the best cultivation methods to improve the quantity and quality of crops while also ensuring those crops reached the market without much waste.

When he took charge of PARC, the main office was in Karachi. Musahib-Ud-Din left his wife and youngest child, Walayet, in Lahore and moved to Karachi alone. Wazir Begum visited him a few times. They felt uncomfortable in this metropolis, the biggest city in the country. They had a hard time dealing with big crowds and the lifestyle of the people. Everyone seemed to be in a rush and stressed out.

Karachi was the capital, but President Ayub Khan had concerns about its location. As a coastal city in the south, he thought Karachi was vulnerable to enemy attacks and potentially tricky to defend. It was the biggest import and export center, and could not simultaneously play the role of capital.

His consultants recommended leaving Karachi as the business hub and moving the functions of the capital to some other part of the country. Thus, on the orders of President Ayub Khan in 1959, the seat of government was moved to Rawalpindi temporarily. Islamabad (Pakistan's current capital) was built from scratch in the vacant fields of the Himalayan foothills. Gradually the offices started moving from Rawalpindi to Islamabad. This beautiful city became the official capital of Pakistan on August 14, 1967.

Photo courtesy of Google Maps

After becoming the head of PARC, Musahib-Ud-Din's office also moved to Islamabad. He worked very hard to get the new center established. Gradually he moved the staff from Karachi to Islamabad and secured new dwellings for them and their families. Another big challenge was to find qualified advisors for the council. He relied on his extensive experience in the field. He also sought help from government and private sectors to accomplish this task.

Musahib-Ud-Din made plans to establish new labs in different parts of the country. He started several new research projects for his scientists to study common crops like wheat, corn and Pearl Millet (Bajra). He was instrumental in importing several successful varieties of crops from other parts of the world. He instructed his staff to do research and determine which were most suitable for Pakistan's climate.

After reaching Islamabad he sent for his wife, and they instantly fell in love with this peaceful city. They appreciated the green grass, plants, and trees. They loved the gentle traffic flow, the spacious home given to them by the Pakistani government, and the relaxed lifestyle.

Walayet remembers the fabulous house in Islamabad where his parents lived. They had servants to take care of the house and the family. He also remembers several big rooms to relax, dine and socialize in. Musahib-Ud-Din was chauffeured around the city and family members occasionally accompanied him.

When Professor and Mrs. Khan were living in Islamabad, Naseem was teaching in a high school in Maryland and Saleem was working under the Royal Ministry of Health in Iran as a general practice physician. Naeem was in Peshawar with her husband and children. Tasneem and Shamim were also married and lived with their husbands in Punjab (the biggest province in Pakistan). They were teaching in colleges of their choice.

Walayet was the only one unmarried. Later, he would become one of only two Pakistani students to win a special merit scholarship to study at the RCD International School of Insurance and Economics in Tehran. There, he studied alongside students from Turkey, Iran, and Pakistan.

Musahib-Ud-Din's new job came with enormous responsibilities. He took them very seriously and did his best to fulfill them. From the beginning, he knew he had to pay attention to the rapidly growing population in the country and their need for an adequate food supply. He encouraged young agriculture scientists to address the issue of possible food shortages in the future. He wholeheartedly supported their ongoing efforts to improve the quantity and quality of different crops in Pakistan.

He always appreciated those Pakistani scientists who worked diligently with Dr. Norman Borlaug. Dr. Borlaug was a visionary. His name has gone down in the history books for his extraordinary contributions to humanity. He received the Nobel Peace Prize for developing a robust wheat strain. He fathered the "green revolution," a series of improved cultivation methods that enabled Pakistan, India, and Mexico to keep pace with their population growth. Musahib-Ud-Din supported those scientists who advocated improved cultivation methods and the new wheat variety developed by Dr. Borlaug.

Khan Sahib took keen interest to learn about the problems the farmers were facing. Along with his staff he did his best to provide them with necessary solutions. He told his staff to teach farmers new techniques and ensure they were implemented correctly. He continued to communicate with agriculture leaders of Pakistan and other countries to discuss best practices.

He recognized another challenge that the farmers were facing. They could grow massive amounts of produce but getting it into kitchens before it spoiled was an infrastructure problem. He addressed this issue by involving the senior government officials willing to help.

He had already begun to travel widely across Pakistan; now, he began to travel internationally. He visited the Philippines, Egypt, Lebanon, Iran, Germany, France, Thailand, and Japan. Not only did he share agriculture practices in Pakistan with the scientists in those countries, but he also learned about theirs. After every foreign trip, he wrote to his government about his recommendations based on the new things he learned abroad.

When he visited Germany, he was enchanted by a piece of technology that would enable the attendees of a conference to understand each other. It was a little device that one would place in the ears. If the user was an English speaker, they would then be able to hear a translation of other languages in English. Whenever representatives from several different countries came together to discuss important issues, this device helped immensely.

Anytime he visited a country, he hit the ground running when it came to the agricultural practices of that area. He wanted to know about topography, soil composition, and how common crops were grown successfully. He spoke with people; he went to the local markets and stopped at roadside stands along the way. After returning to Pakistan, he always wrote up his observations for scientific journals and public interest publications.

CHAPTER FORTY

THE PROBLEM OF THE MANGO TREES

I n the early 1970s, Egyptian mango trees struggled to produce fruit. Most of the mangos would fall from the trees before they were ready. The government of Egypt reached out to the University of Berkeley for help. They requested the university to send an expert to their country who could figure out the problem and make recommendations. The university was pleased to honor the request and asked Professor Musahib-Ud-Din to pay a visit. The university knew of his interest and research concerning mangoes. They even offered to pay for the trip.

Professor Khan told the university he would be delighted to visit Egypt for such a good cause. Thus, in January of 1974, he was invited by the Egyptian government to assist with the production of mango fruits. Once all the formalities were taken care of, he was on his way. He told his family and friends how keen he was to visit Egypt.

Before his trip, he read a book about that country. He learned many interesting facts. He discovered that caliphs who ruled after Prophet Muhammad (PBUH) spread Islam in that part of the world. He also learned that the British controlled Egypt from 1882 to 1922. He had lived under British control, and he had powerful feelings about that experience so he understood how vital autonomy was to Egypt.

When Professor Khan visited Egypt, Anwar Sadat was the President. He was very popular and devoted to bringing significant economic reforms. The problem with the mangoes was distressing everyone.

Musahib-Ud-Din slept on the plane ride to Cairo. He always slept on public transportation and arrived at his destination refreshed. He met the Egyptian diplomats at the airport and rode to the hotel in a state car, as he was accustomed to at that stage of his career.

Along the way, he shouted to the driver to stop when he saw a fruit and vegetable vendor on the shoulder of a two-lane highway. A faded canopy shielded the produce from the sun. An older man with a white beard sat on an overturned bucket, occasionally flicking flies out of his face. He rose when the polished state vehicle pulled over. Musahib-Ud-Din stepped out. The fruit stand offered oranges of varying sizes and heaps of figs and dates.

"Assalamu Alaikum." Khan Sahib started a conversation with the man.

"Walaikum asalam," the vendor responded.

Most Muslims in the world can quote at least a few words of the Quran and say various phrases such as 'Assalamu Alaikum' in Arabic. But for conversational purposes, Musahib-Ud-Din's native language was Urdu, and he could converse in English fluently. "Do you speak English?" he asked.

"A little," the man said.

"Do you grow these fruits yourself?" He wanted to find out.

"No, my brother ," the man said.

"What about the water for farming?" Musahib-Ud-Din wanted to know. When the man looked confused, he tried again, "Where does your brother get the water from?

"Ah yes," The man grasped at the meaning, "From well, but water not much." He went on to demonstrate, using his hands. He raised one flat palm above the other to indicate the method.

Musahib-Ud-Din purchased a bag of oranges and climbed back in the car. On his way to the hotel, they stopped for a meal at the famous Cairo Tower, one of the tallest buildings in the country. One of his Egyptian colleagues showed him the pyramids of Giza from the restaurant where they were enjoying a meal.

The gentleman told his guest, "Thousands of visitors come here regularly and enjoy watching the city of Cairo and nearby pyramids."

The next day, Musahib-Ud-Din's hosts drove him to Giza. Professor Khan was amazed to see the ancient buildings. He thanked his Egyptian colleagues, saying, "I appreciate your hospitality."

Over the next few days, he spoke with several prominent scientists about their mango problem. Accompanied by Egyptian horticulture specialists, he also visited several farms and orchards in different parts of the country to thoroughly examine the trees. He saw some trees with only a few mangoes while many were devoid of their fruits.

After inspecting the farms, he was asked to address a group of scientists to share his observations. He shared his insights and explained why many of the mango trees were having problems. He diagnosed the situation using his knowledge of horticulture and personal research at home. He told his Egyptian colleagues all possible causes of the problems, describing how they could address each one.

At the end of his formal talk, he asked if they had any questions for him. They were impressed by his knowledge and experience and asked him many questions. His prescribed remedies worked and Egypt's mango trees began producing fruit again.

CHAPTER FORTY-ONE

A NEW GRANDSON

After completing his consultation work in Egypt, Musahib-Ud-Din planned to return home. That night he called his wife. "Assalamu Alaikum," he said.

Wazir Begum sounded very excited. With happiness, she started crying, "We have a new grandson!"

Saleem was living in Iran with his wife Sabira, their daughter, and a new baby boy.

"I am thrilled to hear this good news. Is everybody in Saleem's family doing well?" he asked his wife.

"Alhamdulillah. Everyone is fine."

Professor Khan stayed on the phone a little longer to talk with his wife about their other children and the weather back home. As he spoke, he began to consider visiting Iran.

"What do you think if I visit Saleem and his family instead of coming straight home?" he asked.

"I like that idea," his wife answered.

"Please ask someone in my office to contact Saleem." He requested. In those days, ordinary people in Iran didn't have phones, and Saleem's family was no different.

"I think they're still at the hospital. I just got the telegram from Saleem about this happy news," Wazir Begum responded. "I will ask your assistant to contact Saleem."

Khan Sahib hung up and made another phone call to the airline to change his flight. He contacted Saleem's clinic and left a message for his son about his plans. When the travel arrangements were completed, he packed his suitcase and went to bed. In the morning, he headed to the airport to catch his flight. He arrived, bag in hand, ready to board the plane, but the flight was late. There was a snowstorm in Tehran, the likes of which people had not seen in years.

"We had never seen snow before," Saleem said. Almost a foot fell across all of Tehran, grinding traffic to a halt and closing businesses. Drivers used tire chains to drive through the snow, but it mashed the precipitation into a pulpy mess. All vehicles had to crawl down the streets to avoid slipping.

Tehran is one of the biggest cities in the entire continent of Asia. Located near the Caspian Sea, it was about four hours from Borujerd, where Saleem lived with his family. Tehran was the only international airport in the region so Saleem had to make the journey from his house in Borujerd to Tehran to pick up his father. He had no car, so he took a bus. After a long bus ride amid a snowstorm, he finally reached the airport.

He waited at the airport all night, leaving his wife, little daughter, and newborn baby at home alone. His father's plane never came. Without any way to contact his dad, Saleem decided to return home. He arrived on his doorstep, wet and cold. His father was not with him either.

Sabria ushered him inside. "Where is your father?" She peeled Saleem's hat off with one hand, cradling the baby with the other.

"I couldn't find him," Saleem said.

A few hours later, there was a knock on the door. A security guard from Saleem's clinic said he heard a phone ringing. Musahib-Ud-Din was trying to send a message to his son, informing him that he had reached Tehran and was taking a bus to Borujerd. Saleem walked to the bus station, snow soaking his work shoes.

"Saleem!" His father called as he exited the bus.

"Dad." Saleem reached out for his father's suitcase, relieving him of the burden before falling into an embrace. "Thank God you arrived safely!"

His father nodded playfully. The two gentlemen walked back down frozen streets to Saleem's house. Sabria opened the door to usher them in, presenting the little one to his grandfather for praise.

Khan Sahib looked at the baby and commented, "My grandson is handsome like his father. May Allah give him a long and healthy life."

While the grandfather cuddled his grandson, Sabira asked, "Would you like some tea?"

"Yes, please." Saleem peeled his wet coat from his arms, shaking it out in the kitchen.

Saleem's father was curious to know what it was like to live in a country he had never seen before. Saleem explained. "Dad, as you know, I was invited by the Royal Ministry of Health to help Iranians, particularly those living in the villages where health services were poor. After arriving in Iran, they sent me to Shiraz. It is a beautiful city not far from the ancient capital, Persepolis (Takhte Jamshid)."

His father was listening with interest. He asked, "Did you work there for a while?"

"Along with my wife and little daughter, I stayed in Shiraz for about six weeks," Saleem replied. "The health ministry had arranged training for us. Not only did we learn the Persian language, but we also received useful information about the health system in the country."

Musahib-Ud-Din noticed a kerosene heater in the corner of his son's main living area, bringing warmth to the tiny house. He saw it and frowned. He was concerned that the heater might cause indoor pollution. The young family wanted to keep the cold at bay, to keep the baby warm and healthy. But was the heater the solution, or would it negatively affect the growing child? He decided to keep his mouth shut. He would not question Saleem's decision and merely attempted to keep the infant as far away from the device as possible.

After he had gone home to Pakistan, Saleem and Sabria visited the family. Musahib-Ud-Din was delighted to see the child again and healthy.

"I didn't want to tell you at the time," he confessed when he and Saleem were alone, "but I was concerned about that heater."

"What heater?" Saleem asked.

"When I visited you in Iran when the baby was born, you were using a heater," he explained.

"Yes?" Saleem still didn't see the connection.

"I was worried it could harm your baby," he said.

"Oh." Saleem took a sip of mango juice from his glass. He didn't know whether to be touched that his father cared or concerned that he might have unknowingly harmed the child.

"But, all is well." Musahib-Ud-Din ended the conversation.

Saleem finished the last of his juice in one deep swallow.

CHAPTER FORTY-TWO

WORKING IN ISLAMABAD BEFORE RETIREMENT

I n Pakistan, in the early 1970s, the retirement age was 55. At 54, Musahib-Ud-Din started getting hints from his family and friends that he should prepare to retire. Still, the government kept extending his time because he was too valuable.

When the capital moved to Islamabad, the city gleamed with white stone. The government offices, beset with columns and looming facades, faced each other across a newly built boulevard. Prime Minister Zulfikar Ali Bhutto's office was on Embassy Road. It was not far from Musahib-Ud-Din's office in the Pakistan Agriculture Research Council building. Now and then, he received an invitation from the Prime Minister to discuss Pakistan's agricultural issues. By coincidence, they were both students at Berkeley. Mr Bhuto graduated in 1950 and Musahib-Ud-Din in 1952.

In late 1971, Saleem worked in a hospital in Rawalpindi. Soon after starting his new job, Sabira joined him. From time to time, Musahib-Ud-Din and Wazir Begum would visit them and enjoy spending a few days at their son's house. Saleem and his father, like many other Pakistanis, would discuss the politics in the country. Saleem knew how his father liked Prime Minister Zulfikar Ali Bhutto.

One day Musahib-Ud-Din told his son, "I know Mr. Bhutto always did a great job. I liked his plans to give East Pakistan rights to govern itself and distribute all the country's wealth fairly." He also reminded Saleem of the Prime Minister's famous statement: "*We need to heal the wounds.*"

Minister of Agriculture, Malik Khuda Bux Butcha, used to invite Professor Musahib-Ud-Din Khan to his residence, where they would talk about crops in the country. Khan Sahib would take a chauffeured car, a Jeep Grand Wagoneer, to visit the minister. Saleem remembered joining his father on one occasion at the Minister of Agriculture's home. He just sat quietly, not an expert on the subject of agriculture, nor a high-ranking government official like his father. Saleem listened as the men in power spoke of crop yields and providing food for the masses. He sipped tea and only spoke at the end of his visit when the host asked him about his professional work at his hospital.

"It's funny," Musahib-Ud-Din told his son as they drove back to Saleem's home. "When I am at the height of my knowledge, experience, and wisdom, *now* they want me to retire."

He was 59 years old when he finally stepped down.

CHAPTER FORTY-THREE

MOVING BACK TO FAISALABAD

After retirement, Musahib-Ud-Din and his wife packed up their belongings. They moved back to Faisalabad to be closer to their families and the university that gave him his start. He had always remained in touch with faculty and students whose research projects he supervised. He was also keen to reconnect with the staff at Ayub Agriculture Research Institute where he worked as its first fodder botanist and later on served as Director General.

When his career met its distinguished end, the university invited him to come back to teach. They moved into a modest house they designed on land they had purchased when he was still working.

He had a student named Arif, with whom he kept in touch. This student hailed from a family who was involved in the construction business.

Arif once asked Professor Khan, "What are your plans after you retire from the government?"

He quickly responded, "After retirement, I will move back to Faisalabad. My life is here. My family is here. My friends are here."

"Where will you live?" Arif asked.

Khan Sahib inhaled slowly, "I will have to look for a house." All his life he had lived in university provided housing, or other homes granted to him by his position. He didn't have his own home to go back to.

"My family has a construction business," Arif said. "They can help you design your own house."

Professor Khan leaned forward, tapping his fingers on the desk. "I know you may think I am rich. I have certainly been fortunate and able to afford nice things for my family. But the truth is, all my good fortune has been loaned to me by the government."

"Professor," Arif said, "it's no problem. These days there are several different ways people can finance big projects."

While he was still working for the government, Musahib-Ud-Din contracted Arif's family to build a new house. He arranged to take a loan against his retirement account and was able to pay it back over 15 years. It was a one-story ranch house split into five sections. Each section had its entrance.

"There was a hallway..." his grandson Ali said, describing the residence. "Not really a hallway because there was no ceiling, but a narrow space that ran the length of the house. The main door of the building would lead to this space. There were doors to each of five sections." In one of the sections, Wazir Begum's sister lived with her family. They rented other sections out; at times, they were given free of charge to poor students.

Musahib-Ud-Din reserved two sections for himself, his wife, and any children or grandchildren who came to visit.

Ali remembers the neighbor across the street had a water buffalo that they kept chained near the front gate. It was downtown in a busy, well-developed area.

After moving back to Faisalabad, Musahib-Ud-Din visited his alma mater to meet with some colleagues and former students.

"Sir!" Professor Nasir Ali gave his mentor a big hug and spoke. "It is so good to see you after a long time!"

"How have you been, and how is your teaching?" Musahib-Ud-Din asked.

"I am enjoying teaching and working with my students on their research. I learned a lot from you. You helped me in so many ways." Nasir Ali offered him a cup of tea and said, "Why didn't you want to stay longer in Islamabad?"

"I think it was the right time for me to leave that city and return to my roots," he told the younger gentleman.

"Do you have time, or are you busy?" Professor Nasir Ali asked his guest. "I have some students coming soon to discuss their projects. I would like you to stay with me. I believe they will benefit from your experience."

"Of course. I like to talk to students about their studies and research," Musahib-Ud-Din said.

Pretty soon the graduate students entered the office and started talking about their ongoing field experiments and lab work they were involved in.

"So I am researching how common crops can be grown successfully in areas where the soil is dry because of a shortage of water supply," one young man said.

"Professor Khan has written a book on soil composition and testing," Professor Nasir Ali pointed to his guest.

The student turned to Musahib-Ud-Din.

"What region are you interested in?" Musahib-Ud-Din asked.

"Balochistan," the young man answered. "My family lives there, in a small village. Life is hard."

Musahib-Ud-Din nodded. "That would be wonderful if you could find better ways to grow different varieties of crops there."

After their conversation was over, Professor Nasir Ali stood to shake his beloved teacher and mentor's hand. "Have you thought about teaching again?"

Khan Sahib opted for a hug instead. "I am certainly interested in teaching."

Professor Nasir Ali smiled, "People know you and your amazing work. It would be our honor if you decided to join the faculty."

Soon after, Musahib-Ud-Din began the next chapter of his life as Professor Emeritus. Because of his continued love for the study of fruits, he joined the department of horticulture. He started teaching a few classes, giving guest lectures, and proctoring exams. He mentored many undergraduate and graduate students, helping them navigate their studies and research work.

Professor Khan left his alma mater in 1961 when the college became a university. When he returned in 1976, he was very pleased to see how the university had expanded. It became one of the best-rated higher education institutions in the country. They added a school as well to serve the needs of young children of parents who were working there.

One of his former students, who was now a professor, bragged about the university and said, "If a family enrolls their children in a kindergarten program in our university school, these children can continue studying until they earn doctorate degrees right here."

After he moved back to Faisalabad, Khan Sahib would sometimes let students share his home either for free or at a reduced cost. Since he designed the house to have multiple entrances and several apartment-like spaces, it lent itself easily to tenants.

One of his wife's sisters had health issues. Over the years, it became increasingly difficult for her to care for her children. Musahib-Ud-Din and his wife asked her to move into their house along with her son Irshad and daughter Ghazala. They raised these children as if they were their own. During that time, Irshad and Ghazala witnessed their uncle's generosity and acts of kindness towards family members, students, and even strangers. They also learned how people respected him because of his extraordinary knowledge of agriculture sciences and decades of experience in teaching, research, and administration.

Students, researchers, and university teachers frequently consulted him. They appreciated technical advice on soil testing, fodders, fruits, and other issues. He would welcome them into his home, serve them tea and snacks and answer any questions they had.

CHAPTER FORTY-FOUR

GRANDSON VISITING PAKISTAN

A li, Saleem's son, lived in America for most of his life. His father encouraged him to write letters to his grandfather in Faisalabad. The correspondence was in English. Ali knew his grandfather could write and speak English quite well. It was interesting to learn about day-to-day life in Pakistan. After a series of strokes, Musahib-Ud-Din's handwriting became very difficult to read. However, Ali still understood what his grandfather was trying to tell him.

Ali remembered a visit to his grandfather when Khan Sahib sat him down on the couch with a glass of lemonade. He rummaged through his closet and returned with a tin box that might have once held biscuits.

"Look here." Grandfather presented Ali with the box, sitting on the couch beside him.

Ali took the object. He opened the top with a little effort, and inside were all the letters he had ever written to his grandfather. Ali's notes spoke of friends and baseball games dating back to early elementary school. They were mundane but accurate and painted a picture of his entire life; his grandfather had saved them all. Ali at once felt the weight of his grandfather's pride and a blossoming understanding of what family meant to the patriarch.

Ali had visited his grandparents in Faisalabad a few summers when he was growing up. He remembers his cousins getting a scolding from their grandfather for not being on top of their classes consistently. "I think my sister and I got off easy because we didn't see our grandparents that often. We used to visit them from far away," Ali said.

Whenever the grandchildren visited from the U.S., grandfather kept a close eye on what they were drinking or eating. He knew very well that the grandchildren were at risk of an upset stomach because the water and foods in Pakistan were unfamiliar. He would ensure they only drank water which was boiled and then left overnight to cool. He used to tell them, "Because you are visiting from the U.S., your belly may not be able to handle the bacteria in the tap water here."

He was also concerned about street food or different cooking techniques or ingredients. He did not want his grandchildren to suffer from any illness related to water or food, so he monitored their intake. They ate home-cooked meals and fresh fruits exclusively. Ali remembered his grandfather even preventing them from overeating. As a child, he thought this much attention was overbearing. Still, he did admit that they never got sick during their visits to their grandparents in Pakistan.

Ali has fond memories of taking the train to Peshawar with his grandparents to visit his aunt Naeem and her family. They also went to Lahore to see another set of relatives. Ali always loved being with his cousins whenever he visited Pakistan. He thought it was a lot of fun.

Ali liked visiting the university with his grandfather. "He would pop into offices to say hello to people," Ali said. "And I remember a garden in front of one building, where they were conducting some kind of experiment with different growing conditions." His grandfather had stopped to examine the tomatoes growing in the test plots and chatted with a student taking notes on a clipboard.

Now and then, they wrote letters to each other. His grandfather even sent a telegram once when Ali graduated from high school. Ali had never received a telegram before. It came from the local post office, written on a manila card. He did not understand what it was, but he was very excited to receive a congratulatory urgent message from across the oceans sent by his beloved grandfather. He shared this telegram with his family and friends and told them how happy he was to receive it.

Ali approached his father with the idea of visiting Pakistan on his own. He was out of college and was waiting to start medical school. It seemed like the perfect time to go traveling.

"Where would you like to go in Pakistan?" Saleem asked.

Ali shrugged. "I've never been up north."

"Okay," Saleem said. He called his father later that week to share what his son Ali wished to do.

"I'll go with him," Musahib-Ud-Din was quick to say. He made a few phone calls to people he knew: friends, and family. He lined up some hotels, rented a car, and paid a young man to drive. When Ali arrived in Faisalabad, the trip was all set.

They climbed into the back seat and drove from Faisalabad to Peshawar, where they picked up Naeem's husband, Anwar. They spent the night in Naeem's home and enjoyed delicious dishes and bread that Naeem specially made for them. After dinner, Naeem served fruit for dessert and then again for breakfast because she knew her father's habits so well. The four men left Naeem's home early in the morning to drive to Islamabad.

On the way up to the mountains, the driver pulled the car over to rest for a moment. The passengers stepped out of the car to stretch their legs. The view was majestic. In the distance, they could see the mountains, their sharp cliffs puncturing the glaciers. By the roadside, green vegetation clung to steep hills. The air was cold.

"Do you know what this plant is?" Ali's grandfather picked a weed from beside the car.

Ali narrowed his eyes. He had a suspicion that the plant his grandfather held aloft was marijuana.

"I don't know," Ali said.

"It's cannabis," his grandfather told him. "It grows wild here."

"Oh," Ali said. He was standing on a hill full of marijuana, on a road trip with his grandfather. Musahib-Ud-Din discarded the plant as soon as they finished their conversation and climbed back into the car. Ali exhaled the breath he had been holding and tried not to laugh as he followed his grandfather.

As they drove, Musahib-Ud-Din told Ali about his work. Not the work he had done for the government, but the position *after* the government. He talked about the students he mentored, his guest lectures, and his English classes for young children.

"I guess your retirement will be posthumous," Ali said. It seemed like a joke, but as soon as the words were out of his mouth, Ali regretted them. He started thinking it might have been better to say his grandfather would never retire instead of making a joke about death.

Musahib-Ud-Din laughed. "I like it," he said. "You should get a prize for this unique idea." Grandfather's comments made Ali feel somewhat relaxed.

Wazir Begum's mother had once said that she had seen other people deteriorate after retirement. "But your husband has defeated retirement." She told her daughter. "It has not affected him at all."

"Why did you study agriculture?" Ali asked.

"That's what was available," his grandfather quickly answered. "I was able to get a scholarship to the College of Agriculture, so I studied agricultural sciences."

"You didn't always want to go into agriculture?" Ali was puzzled. "In the United States, children are encouraged to study what makes them happy."

"I wanted an education," the grandfather said. "A good education is crucial because it helps determine your future success."

When they reached Islamabad, Musahib-Ud-Din showed his grandson around. They drove up to an overlook to see the city spread out in the valley before them. "That was my office, right there." He pointed to the center cluster, to the bright white buildings on either side of a boulevard. "And over there, the Prime Minister's office."

They spent the night in a hotel and ate a meal at a nearby restaurant. Professor Khan usually avoided eating mass-prepared food. He preferred to eat at home. But since there were no cooking facilities for the visiting guests in the hotel and the food that his daughter Naeem had packed for them was dwindling, he agreed to have a meal out. However, he would not compromise on his bedtime schedule, so the little party was asleep by 10 p m.

The next day, they were going to visit Rawalpindi. Musahib-Ud-Din was happy to note Ali's interest in the city and its people. He explained that the location was a military base in the early years after Partition. Ali's grandfather told him he was very fond of President Ayub Khan, who built Islamabad near the city they were about to visit.

Wazir Begum's younger sister, Ameer Begum, lived in Rawalpindi. The four men made the short drive from their hotel and wound through the ancient streets. As the driver parked the car, Ali gathered himself to climb out.

His grandfather pulled him back. "Here." He pressed a folded wad of bills into Ali's hand. It was at least one hundred rupees. "This is for the family maid," he instructed his grandson quietly.

Ali followed his grandfather through the doorway into a modest living room. They were greeted warmly by Ameer Begum. The conversation was in Urdu, and while Ali was familiar with the language, he wasn't fluent. After a few minutes, the family's maid came out with a tray, setting down little bowls of homemade curries and loaves of bread. She arranged everything nicely on the coffee table. The gentlemen crowded around to eat.

Ali rose to his feet and followed the maid back into the kitchen. He gave her the money that his grandfather had designated. She smiled and blushed, grateful for the unexpected gesture. Ali acknowledged her thanks with a big smile, rejoined his grandfather at the table, and ate a meal far better than the one they had the night before.

After this family visit, they started traveling north. On their way, they stopped at several tourist attractions and enjoyed the beauty of nature. The scenes all around were so captivating, the likes of which Ali never had a chance to observe elsewhere. Wherever they went, he was surprised to see hundreds of tourists.

Anwar shared many interesting facts about the areas they visited. They spent a night in a hotel and took their evening tea on the porch. His uncle spoke as they looked out over the beautiful flowers, lush green trees, mountains, and clear spring water. "Ali, I often visit these areas to research medicinal plants. I will write a few papers about my observations and submit them to a couple of research journals for publication."

Ali appeared mesmerized, watching the extraordinary natural beauty all around him. The next day it was time for them to go back to Peshawar.

When Ali returned from the road trip with his grandfather, he was impressed with the older man's memory. His grandfather shared detailed information at every point in their journey, in every village they traveled through, and every cultural icon they saw. He knew the history of the region, the politics behind buildings, and the names of prominent diplomats in the area.

"How was your trip?" Saleem asked his son when Ali returned home to America.

"Grandpa has a photographic memory," was the first thing Ali said. After he and his father shared a laugh, he described the vacation in more detail. "I didn't know the northern region of Pakistan approaches the Himalayan mountains. It is certainly the most beautiful part of the country. No wonder so many tourists visit from around the world every year."

After listening carefully to Ali, Saleem said, "I am glad you liked the places you saw. Credit certainly goes to you; it was your idea." Then he took a deep breath and continued, "I wish I were there with you too. I never got a chance to see that beautiful region of Pakistan. In school, we learned about K2, the second-highest mountain on earth. We also read about the famous Kaghan valley and its lovely lakes. Everyone loved talking about beautiful Hunza valley, where people are known for longevity, many of them reaching the age of one hundred years."

CHAPTER FORTY-FIVE

A FAVORITE STUDENT

O ver the years, many students benefited from the guidance provided to them by their mentor, Professor Musahib-Ud-Din Khan. A few of them built close relationships with him and cherished their friendship. One of those students was Dr. Habib-Ur-Rehman. He studied under Musahib-Ud-Din for his Master's degree and researched medicinal plants. Later, he became a teacher at the Punjab Agricultural College, now called the Agriculture University of Faisalabad. He went to Canada and received his doctorate in Plant Genetics. For five years, he and Musahib-Ud-Din were colleagues. Later, Dr. Habib started working at Peshawar University but kept in touch throughout Musahib-Ud-Din's stint in high-position government jobs.

Dr. Habib remembers traveling to agriculture conferences with his mentor. "We went to Lahore and Karachi," Habib recalls. About the meetings, he also remembers, "The conferences featured many different scientific topics. The hotel served food, and transportation was always by train. People didn't have cars back then."

After retirement, Musahib-Ud-Din and his wife often made the day-long trip from Faisalabad to visit their oldest daughter Naeem and her family in Peshawar. Whenever they were in Peshawar, Dr. Habib would pay a visit to Professor Khan, who would ensure quality time with his favorite student. They would talk about several different topics like their research interests, the latest developments in the field, and life back home in Faisalabad.

One day when Dr. Habib was visiting, he saw Professor Musahib-Ud-Din enjoying the company of his grandchildren. He looked at them fondly and commented, "Khan Sahib, these children are brilliant. They know a lot about the history of Peshawar."

Professor Khan liked what he heard about his grandchildren and asked them, "What have you learned about Peshawar in your school?"

His grandson Jawad said, "Nana, our teacher told us that Peshawar is the oldest city in Pakistan. It is at least 3,000 years old."

Then Dr. Habib looked at his professor's granddaughter, Sadia, and said, "Is there anything you want to tell your Nana?"

She was eager to share something interesting, "Over the centuries, Alexander the Great, the Aryans, and the Moguls all came through Khyber Pass to our historic city."

At this point, Aliya, the middle granddaughter, jumped in, "Nana, we can all go with you and Nani to see the Khyber Pass. The town of Landi Kotal is right there. We can buy nice things, and we do not have to pay customs duty either."

Their grandmother could easily sense the excitement. She walked into the living room and asked, "What are you all talking about?"

Munaza appeared excited, "Nani, we will all go to Landi Kotal tomorrow with you and Nana."

Everyone started laughing.

When asked to describe Musahib-Ud-Din as a professor, Dr. Habib had only good things to say. "He was very popular because he took a keen interest in his students and was always happy to help them. We would listen to his lectures and perform experiments under his supervision in our laboratory." While working on his Master's degree, he would often visit his professor's residence in the evenings to receive guidance and feedback about his ongoing research. Habib was also among those students invited to Professor Khan's home for special holidays.

Chapter Forty-Six

PROFESSOR EMERITUS

L iving in the city's heart, Musahib-Ud-Din commuted to the
university on his bicycle. He could have used his savings to buy a car
but he preferred the simple life, exercise, a bike afforded him. Multiple
times his children urged him to purchase more dignified transportation.
They even offered to buy him a nice car. He shrugged them off, explaining
that he did not need to show off.

He structured his days as he had always done. It didn't matter that he had
no monumental meetings to attend or big budgets to oversee anymore. He
was a man of habit. He had a daily routine, and he stuck to it.

In the mornings, he would wake up before dawn, wash his hands, face, and
feet as Muslims must do before prayer. After this cleansing ritual (called
Wudu), he would perform *Fajr*, the dawn prayer. Then he and his wife
would go back to sleep for another hour until the sun lit the sky. The
couple would take a stroll around the neighborhood as soon as it was light
enough.

Back home, he would make tea for the two of them. He would have a healthy breakfast, including half a grapefruit, that he would eat with a special spoon. He would leave his wife to do housework or visit her sister and take his bike to the university. He held open office hours for students seeking advice when he was not giving lectures or proctoring exams.

Early afternoons he would return home and have lunch with his wife. After that, he would nap for about an hour and insist everyone in the house do the same. In the evenings, he opened his home to students and young researchers to consult him about anything they wanted to discuss.

As Professor Emeritus, Musahib-Ud-Din had access to every corner of the university. He taught undergraduate classes regularly and mentored students at every level, from undergraduate to doctoral. He continued to stay abreast of innovations in the field. He constantly enlightened himself by reading the latest world literature. His correspondence with other scientists was legendary.

One morning, he swung by the university mail room. His box was full of letters and journals. "Asalamu alaikum Khan Sahib," the graduate student staffing the mail room called out.

"Walaikum assalam," Khan Sahib replied with a smile.

With all his mail, he went to the office of a former student, who was now an assistant professor. He put the envelopes on the desk and began to open one.

The younger man looked at Professor Khan and asked, "Why do you always get so much mail?"

Musahib-Ud-Din shrugged. "I write letters to many people."

The young man smiled. "What are these letters you received today?"

"Dear Professor Khan," he read aloud, "Thank you for your recent article on the nutritional value of citrus fruits." He paused, lowering the letter, "In one scholarly journal, I read an article which I translated into simple Urdu and sent to a newspaper. The editor wrote this letter to thank me."

"And the rest?" Impressed, the young man gestured at the rest of the mail.

Khan Sahib pawed through the pile, glancing at the return addresses. "This one is from Florida. I have been corresponding with the agriculture scientists of the Citrus Research Institute for a while now. This one is from a former student. He is an expert in plant genetics. I have been following his research."

"Okay." The other man laughed. "You'll have to forgive me for thinking you would never slow down."

Musahib-Ud-Din also visited Ayub Agriculture Research Institute regularly. He had fond memories of working with the staff there. Many people knew him well, either they were his former students or worked under him. They loved his visits. They would request him to have a cup of tea with them, taking the opportunity to discuss their ongoing research and ask him for his thoughts about future projects.

A few scientists reminded him of the time when he served as the Director General of Ayub Institute and encouraged the institute and the university to collaborate and publish their joint work in prestigious journals.

After retirement, he started a tutoring center to teach neighborhood children math and English. His granddaughter Mamoona recalled one story he often told these young students.

SALEEM A. KHAN, M.D.

His First Flight, by Liam O'Flaherty, is a story included in many language-learning courses. Students to whom Professor Khan read this story were studying English as a foreign language. In the story, a young seagull is too afraid to fly. He sees his brothers and sisters, who have smaller wings, leap successfully into the air and fly away. But he remains too scared to try. His parents become angry with him, but he still does not try to fly. Eventually, he is left in the nest by himself. After a day, his mother comes back with a fish in her mouth. She does not deliver the fish to her baby. Instead, she throws it into the air. Now the little hungry seagull leaps over the cliff to catch it and starts flying.

Professor Khan's young students gathered on couches in his living room, listening intently as their teacher narrated the story. After several tellings, they could anticipate when the teacher's voice would rise and fall, and they cheered for the little seagull every time.

"My grandfather loved telling that story again and again," Mamoona said. "He believed that only through struggle could there be any success. He would always say that parents sometimes have to be strict to be kind."

In his retirement years, his youngest daughter Shamim would visit him with her family every now and then. Her daughter, Nadia, remembered eating different varieties of mangoes, when she saw her grandparents. She also remembered how her grandfather would make pickled mangoes that he would preserve in big jars and share with family and at times with neighbors.

Naeem remembered the head of the chemistry department at the University of Peshawar saying, "I have never seen an old man like your father in Pakistan who is so aware of the latest scientific developments."

The faculty members he worked with as Professor Emeritus said they respected Professor Khan because he knew the agriculture problems of Pakistan like the back of his hand and he could deliver lectures on different topics at a moment's notice.

Chapter Forty-Seven

ALI'S WEDDING

Saleem eventually settled in Delaware and became a founding member of the most prominent Islamic center in the state. He worked as a child/adolescent psychiatrist at a local hospital and at an outpatient clinic for children, youth, and their families.

When Musahib-Ud-Din came to Delaware to attend his grandson Ali's wedding, he wanted to learn more about the state. "It was the first state to ratify the constitution," Saleem said. "It is also the second smallest state in the country." He told his father about lovely beaches in Delaware on the Atlantic Ocean. Musahib-Ud-Din then asked about farming in Delaware. Saleem knew agriculture was significant for his father. He thought for a moment and then said, "Southern parts of the state are full of farms. They grow corn, wheat, barley, and fruits. Chickens are also an important commodity."

Saleem told of one instance when his father was visiting him in Delaware. Musahib-Ud-Din had written a letter to one of his Florida colleagues. Due to a series of strokes, it became hard for him to write, and reading what he had committed to paper was difficult. He was aware of this issue. He wanted the letter typed so that his friend could read it easily.

Saleem was almost out the door; he had his jacket on, briefcase in hand. He grabbed his lunch from the counter where his wife, Sabria, had left it.

Musahib-Ud-Din sat at the kitchen table, writing. He put his pen down and handed a paper to Saleem, "Son."

"Yes, Dad?" Saleem turned toward his father quickly.

"Can you get this typed?" He knew that Saleem had a secretary at work who could type it.

"Sure." Saleem accepted the paper. He scanned it absently, then folded it into his briefcase. "How urgent is it?"

"Not urgent," he told his son, "When you come home, just bring it back with you."

Saleem muffled a smile behind a cough. Running late, he hurried out the door and into the car. He dumped his lunch and briefcase into the passenger seat and pulled out of the driveway. When he arrived at work, he paused at his secretary's desk.

"Excuse me, Susan." Saleem opened his briefcase. "Can you have this typed?"

"Sure." She accepted the letter and placed it down in her inbox.

"It's...important," Saleem said. "It's not work-related, but it's for my father. He would like it done by the end of business today."

Susan blinked. She stared at Saleem, trying to judge whether he was being serious.

Saleem broke into a smile. "He's...he was a high-ranking official in Pakistan. He's used to having a staff and getting things done immediately."

"Oh." Susan nodded, "I get it." She saved the document she was working on and immediately switched to his father's letter. "Dr. Khan," She said later, when she turned over the typed missive, "We all thought you were pushy, but your father, I don't think I can work under him. I would not be able to keep up with his speed."

In one of his professional responsibilities, Musahib-Ud-Din was a fruit specialist. He had researched grapefruits at the University of California, Berkeley, and worked on kinnows for several years in Pakistan. After he retired from the responsibility of his government job, he began to communicate with fruit specialists in Florida.

These scientists were researching all kinds of citrus fruits and had run across Musahib-Ud-Din's research. He was interested in their pioneering work in the field, which led him to reaching out and the conversation continued for many years. He would read their latest research with a lot of interest and give his feedback. From time to time, he would receive letters from them. When visiting his family in the United States, he insisted on making a trip to Florida.

It was a happy occasion. His grandson Ali was getting married. Saleem met his father at the airport.

"How was your flight, Father?" Saleem asked after retreating from their hug.

"Alhamdulillah (thank God)," Musahib-Ud-Din said.

He planned not only to attend the wedding of his grandson but also to visit as many family members and friends as he could on this trip. Saleem brought his father back to his home in Delaware. His son Ali's wedding was to be in Las Vegas, where his future in-laws were living. As they were enjoying a dinner prepared by Saleem's wife, his father said, "I have never been to Las Vegas. Why do people wish they could see this city at least once in their lifetime?"

Saleem looked at his wife and then responded to his father, "Dad, it is a big tourist destination because it is full of fine restaurants, hotels and casinos."

Saleem also told his father that the city had become a place where many people come for a memorable wedding.

When his father heard about drive-through weddings, he laughed and said, "Really? I never knew that."

Musahib-Ud-Din was also curious as to why Las Vegas was called Sin City.

Saleem sat back in his chair, looked at his wife again, and told his father, "Dad, there is a lot of gambling; at times, gamblers lose everything. Alcohol consumption is problematic; many people get drunk and embarrass themselves."

Las Vegas was several hours away by air from Saleem's house, and it was also in the middle of a desert. It was sweltering that summer. It was so hot that many relatives complained they couldn't stand outside for more than a few minutes without getting a headache. Musahib-Ud-Din didn't seem to be bothered.

"I think you should stay here," Saleem told his father. Delaware had a much more temperate climate.

"No," his father quickly responded.

"Father, it is very hot." Saleem tried again.

"I came all the way from Pakistan to see Ali getting married." The father was adamant.

"But…" Saleem wanted to explain how worried he was about his father's health. He was an older gentleman, and he had been through so much. At times he seemed fragile.

"Don't worry," Musahib-Ud-Din said. "I will be fine."

He was, in fact, better able to deal with the heat than almost any other wedding guest.

CHAPTER FORTY-EIGHT
VISITING FLORIDA

After grandson Ali's wedding, Musahib-Ud-Din went to Indiana with his youngest child Walayet, who was teaching finance at a university. Soon after the father and son disembarked from the plane, Walayet's wife greeted them at the airport with a big smile and hugged both gentlemen. She held her husband's hand as they returned to the car. Everyone climbed inside, and after making sure her father-in-law was comfortable, she started driving them home.

While driving to Walayet's home, his father commented, "I saw many big fields full of crops."

His son agreed with his observation and said, "Dad, you are right. Our state is known for its farmland and agriculture. Our farmers grow a lot of corn and send it to other states too."

They talked about Indiana until Walayet's wife pulled into their driveway.

Once seated at the kitchen table, with glasses of lemonade to go around, Musahib-Ud-Din straightened. "How far is it to Florida from here by car?" he asked.

Walayet and his wife exchanged a glance. "Two days?" Walayet guessed.

"Two days," his wife confirmed.

"Why?" Walayet was almost afraid to ask.

"I would like to visit the Citrus Research and Education Center. It is in Lake Alfred, Florida." Musahib-Ud-Din told them.

Walayet blinked. He looked to his wife for backup. "It's very hot," he said.

His father waited for a better excuse.

"It's a long drive." Walayet tried again.

"I have corresponded with the Citrus Research Center scientists for many years. They have read my research, I read theirs. I am here now. I would like to meet my colleagues and see their facilities."

Later that night, Walayet phoned his brother Saleem. "Dad wants me to drive him to Florida," Walayet said.

"You can't," Saleem responded.

"I have to," Walayet said.

"What did you say?" Saleem asked.

"I said okay," Walayet sighed.

"You have to think about Dad's health," Saleem reasoned, "It's so hot, and it's such a long drive. I don't think it would be good for him."

"Would you like to talk to him?" Walayet threatened, "Would you like me to put him on the phone?"

Back home in Delaware, Saleem put his head down on the arm of the sofa. He did not know what to say. He just listened to his brother patiently.

"I'll call you when we get there," Walayet promised.

Walayet had the honor of driving his father to Florida. They spent two days on the road and one night in a hotel. On the second day, it rained, and Walayet could barely see past the windshield wipers. He had to stop driving.

When the rain stopped, they started again. They were driving down a four-lane stretch of highway, halfway between Florida and the western border of Georgia, when Musahib-Ud-Din spotted a vegetable and fruit stand.

"Pull over!" he almost yelled.

Walayet did as he was told, turning his car off the highway just beyond the striped blue and white tent. Before Walayet could say anything, his father unbuckled his seatbelt and leaped from the car.

"Wait–" Walayet struggled with his seatbelt, finally getting out of the car. He followed his father, feeling the hot sun rays on his skin. He hustled over to the vegetable and fruit stand, where his father was already looking at several different kinds of seasonal vegetables and fruits.

"How are you all doing today?" the vendor asked.

"Fine, thanks. Hope you are doing fine too." Walayet said.

Musahib-Ud-Din smiled. Now that the storm had passed, he took his time perusing the offerings. There were crates of peaches, apples, and oranges. There were also tomatoes, cucumbers, and bell peppers for sale.

"Come, take a picture," he asked his son with the gesture of his hand.

"Is it okay if I take a few pictures?" Walayet asked the vendor.

The man smiled and said, "Go ahead."

Walayet took photos of his father standing next to different vegetables and fruits. They purchased a small bag of peaches and then walked back to their car.

Finally, they reached Florida and Musahib-Ud-Din spent time with the scientists he had corresponded with for many years. They shared information with him about the latest research projects they were involved in. He also asked a couple of scientists about the possibility of developing seedless kinnow in the US. The Florida scientists were excited to meet the professor, who was well versed in the newest research on citrus fruits.

They excitedly showed him and his son around their facilities, including outside fields and indoor labs. Walayet drove back home after two days; the trip took them almost a week from Indiana to Florida. When he finally called his brother Saleem to tell him they had arrived home safely, the elder brother breathed a sigh of relief.

CHAPTER FORTY-NINE
WAZIR BEGUM

Musahib-Ud-Din knew how lucky he was to have married and fallen in love with a dedicated woman like Wazir Begum. He used to admire her long hair, telling his children and grandchildren what a beautiful woman she was. During his active professional life, he was too busy. His wife managed the house with the help of a maid and a couple of servants. After his retirement, he helped her with the household chores as much as possible. He consulted her for every move he made, from furthering his education to accepting any new job offers in different parts of the country.

Their granddaughter, Mamoona, did not have to go to school on Fridays because when she was growing up, schools were closed on that day. She knew it was a day off for her grandfather from his university too. Whenever possible, she would visit her grandparents on Fridays.

One day when visiting from Lahore, she sat on the floor in the living room beside the couch, coloring in a book. She selected her favorite colors and started working on a page. Her grandfather sat beside her, trying to figure out a newspaper puzzle while her grandmother cooked lunch. Mamoona always loved such moments together and still talks about them.

The smell of coriander bit the air, and soon Mamoona and Grandfather could smell onions frying.

He leaned forward and said, "Your grandmother is amazing. She is always busy doing something around the house and making everyone feel happy. My life would be incomplete without her."

"What's that?" Wazir Begum poked her head around the dividing wall, hearing her name.

"I was telling Mamoona how fortunate I am to have you in my life and how I love you so much," her husband said.

She smiled and went back to her cooking.

She was kind to everyone. Her grandchildren remember her as being gentle and affectionate. Even when their grandfather was strict and chided them about grades, Wazir Begum balanced his anger with calm. She supported her husband in every venture, from research and teaching to administrative responsibilities. She rallied the family around them, helping both children and grandchildren. She also treated all the siblings, aunts, and uncles on both sides of the family with respect and kindness.

"Out of love, my grandmother used to call me 'camel' because I was taller than my sisters," Munaza said. Munaza is the daughter of Naeem, the oldest daughter of Wazir Begum. She used to visit her grandparents at least once a year. Her grandparents loved Munaza's visits to their home in Faisalabad. Playfully, Wazir Begum would tell her granddaughter not to come to her kitchen.

"Stay out of my kitchen." The grandmother laughed, shaking a towel at Munaza, "You are going to break something."

Saleem remembers his mother being a serious woman who wouldn't tell jokes or funny stories but would certainly enjoy them when someone else told them. She was an intelligent woman, but she never had a chance to finish school because of the traditions of the time. She was down-to-earth, sincere, and loving.

After her children had grown and her husband had retired from government, they lived in the modest house they built in Faisalabad. It was undoubtedly a time of adjustment for them. They had grown accustomed to living in big homes with chauffeur-driven vehicles at their disposal.

One day Wazir Begum came home from the market. She saw a woman and her daughter begging in the street in front of her house.

"Please, ma'am," the woman held out dirty hands, her eyes showing behind a thin black veil. Her little girl clung to her legs, eyes cast down, hair in a tangled mess. "In the name of Allah, can you give me some money, please?"

"Come in," Wazir Begum said.

She led the pair through the main entrance, down the open-air hallway, to her residence in the back. She went into her kitchen and gave them curry and bread from the lunch she had prepared for herself and her husband.

She found an extra pair of socks and a nice shirt in the closet. She gave them to the little girl, making her very happy. Then she brought a new comb and told the mother to work out the child's knots. The woman came back a few more times, and Wazir Begum would invite her in each time.

Naeem often tells her friends a story about her mother that left a lasting impression on her mind. One day a neighborhood woman visited her mother, telling her about her husband's sudden death. With tears in her eyes, she said, "I have no source of income. Instead of going to school, I am afraid my four-year-old son will be begging on the streets with me."

Wazir Begum knew her quite well. After listening to the woman, she encouraged her to start working as a maid and stop thinking about begging. She also gave her a notebook and a pencil and said, "Start teaching your son the alphabet and numbers."

The woman followed Wazir Begum's suggestions. Occasionally she would stop by and brag about her son's educational achievements. When her son was a grown up man, she came back to visit Wazir Begum again and told her how thankful she was, "Because of your advice, I did not go to the streets to beg, instead I started working. I also kept encouraging my son to excel in school. When you gave me a notebook and a pencil for him, I could not imagine a day would come when he would go to America on a full scholarship to study for his PhD."

Wazir Begum smiled and hugged the woman.

"Growing up," Saleem recalled, "we often thought that she was an angel in the form of a human being."

One evening when the children were young, they witnessed a conflict between their mother and father. "I don't know what it was about," Saleem said, "but it was rare to see our mother that angry."

She threw down her apron and raised a finger to her husband. She began to speak loudly, not yelling but clearly indicating her displeasure.

"We thought Dad would lose it." Saleem laughed. "We were all afraid."

But Musahib-Ud-Din listened carefully to what his wife said, absorbing every word. When he spoke, he was calm, validating her feelings, and very supportive of her. He said almost nothing, reserving his comments to, "I understand. You are right."

When Saleem asked his father about that conversation years later, Musahib-Ud-Din explained it like this. "In any interaction, things will get worse if two individuals raise their voices simultaneously. If my wife starts getting upset, I keep my mouth shut."

This deference for her feelings served the couple well in their more than fifty years of marriage.

Wazir Begum shared a morning walk with her husband regularly for many years. One morning, they ambled their familiar route, down the street, to the left at the first intersection. They started talking about death.

He took a deep breath and then looked at his wife. Very calmly, he said to her, "I know it is tough to talk about your own death while you are still alive, but we know one day we will all die. I think our children should be prepared. When that day comes, they should not panic."

He was never shy about death. He lived his life as if he would die any day, every decision weighed against the necessity of providing for his family. His wife understood and appreciated this acceptance of the inevitable, but she was worried.

She quietly said, "If something happens to one of us, who will do all the work and who will take care of the children?"

He listened patiently to all her worries and then commented, "The children are grown."

"They still need their parents." She watched the pavement slip away beneath her feet.

He gently said, "Your place will be assured in Jannah (heaven) and inshallah (God willing) , I will be there with you."

In Islam, the belief in the afterlife is similar to Christianity. There is a heaven called Jannah. But souls don't go directly there; they wait, asleep, until Judgment Day. On Judgment Day, God will decide who goes to heaven and who goes to hell. On that day, the prophets will advocate for their followers to be pardoned and allowed to enter heaven. According to Islamic practices, family and friends pray for the deceased when a loved one passes away, saying, "May Allah grant them the highest place in Jannah."

Wazir Begum accompanied her husband on a couple of trips to the United States to visit their children, but not the final one with its road trip to Florida. She passed away in the holy month of Ramadan. She did not suffer an extended illness. After a few days in a hospital, she passed away peacefully in her sleep at her home with her loved ones around her.

Chapter Fifty

Sher Muhammed and Fazalunnisa

They had a little house in Faisalabad, not far from Musahib-Ud-Din's home. Many relatives from both sides of the family also lived in the same neighborhood. They had their own little Panipat (the ancestral city in India) in the space of a few blocks, like a relocated town.

Sher Muhammed spent a lot of time praying, reciting the Holy Quran, and preaching the teachings of Islam to family and friends. His wife kept the house in order, doing many things by herself. She welcomed her grandchildren whenever they were able to visit. When they were grown, she looked forward to seeing her great-grandchildren.

Sher Muhammed was never sick. In all his life, he never even took one aspirin. He was almost ninety years old but still healthy until the day he collapsed on the bedroom floor.

Fazalunnisa shrieked when she found him on the floor. She rushed toward him to check what happened to him. He was still breathing, but she couldn't wake him up. She ran to the neighbors (her niece and nephew) and begged them to come quickly.

The nephew dashed to their home where Sher Muhammed lay, while his wife helped Fazalunnisa dial the phone to her son.

"Musahib," she said quickly.

Musahib-Ud-Din tried to say Islamic greetings , but she cut him off.

"Musahib I can not handle it. Please rush"

"Mother, what happened?"

"Your father fell. He is not responding to us. I need you to be here with me."

He dropped his newspaper and ran out into the street. He flagged a taxi and took the short trip to his parent's house. "Wait here." He gave the taxi driver a folded stack of rupees.

"Yes, sir." The driver nodded.

Khan Sahib hurried inside. His mother paced the kitchen floor crying, her hands wrapped around her arms.

"Oh, Musahib," She started sobbing, diving into his arms.

"Your father fell. He is not talking at all."

Musahib-Ud-Din rushed to join his cousin at his father's side. Sher Muhammed lay on the floor beside his prayer rug in the courtyard of his home. Khan Sahib crouched to check for a pulse but it was feeble.

"Abba?" he called his father. There was no response.

Like many other people in Pakistan, Professor Khan was uncomfortable using the services of an ambulance. From personal experience, he felt it did not function well, and the service was often slow to respond. It was time to act quickly and make sure his father reached the hospital as soon as possible.

"I have a taxi outside," he told his cousin.

The cousin nodded. Together, they lifted Sher Muhammed and maneuvered the older gentleman through the kitchen door. They struggled down the front walkway towards the waiting cab. The cab driver leaped out of his vehicle to open the door, allowing Musahib-Ud-Din and his cousin to lift his father into the back seat. He hopped into the front as the driver took his seat.

"The hospital emergency room." He told the cab driver.

The taxi did its job, and the driver pulled up to the emergency entrance at the hospital. Musahib-Ud-Din leaped out, rounded up a nurse with a gurney, and helped lift his father from the back seat. He stayed with him while the hospital staff wheeled the patient into the examination room. At that point, one of the nurses put a hand up to stop him.

"Please wait here," she demanded.

He halted his forward momentum. He wanted to know his father was still breathing and his heart was beating. He wanted to be with him on the final leg of his journey. But he could not. He turned away and began to pace the hall. After a long moment, he drew a breath to calm himself and sat down to wait.

About twenty minutes later, a doctor came to the area where Musahib-Ud-Din was pacing. "Professor Khan?" he said.

"Yes?" Khan Sahib replied anxiously.

"I am sorry to tell you we could not save your father. He passed away shortly after arrival at the hospital." The doctor softened his voice, attempting to convey empathy.

Musahib-Ud-Din sat still for a while. Tears started flowing down his cheeks as he felt the loss. As soon as he could, he returned to his mother's home to give her the sad news.

She collapsed into his arms, her sorrow so great, she couldn't speak for a long time. Musahib-Ud-Din wrapped his mother in a strong hug, allowing her to grieve for the man who had supported her for so long.

Fazalunnisa lived for several years after her husband's death. Unlike Sher Muhammed, she had some health problems, including high blood pressure, for which she took medication. Living alone was hard for her. She was able to keep the house, and she could still count on relatives living close by, but nights felt very long without her husband.

Every now and then she would stay a few days at her son Musahib-Ud-Din's home. From time to time she would also visit her other grown-up children. One day when she was at her daughter Meraj's house, she said that she was not feeling well.

Meraj offered her a cold drink and requested her to rest in bed. While in bed, she closed her eyes and a few minutes later, stopped breathing. She died peacefully with her family around her. She was laid to rest in the graveyard with all the family members who had gone before.

A few years later, Musahib-Ud-Din and his son Saleem visited the graves. It was autumn and leaves were falling like confetti across the ground.

"I want to be buried here," Musahib-Ud-Din said. "Just make a little room for me."

"Abba, don't talk like that," Saleem said.

His father chuckled. "We all die one day, Son."

Saleem said nothing.

"My father," Musahib-Ud-Din said, staring down at the inscribed headstone. "He did not express his affection in front of others. It's hard to show affection, you know; you are told that's not masculine."

Saleem nodded.

"My father never said, 'I love you.' But at night, when we were sleeping, he would come into our rooms, and give us each a kiss on the forehead." His voice became raw. "That's how I knew he loved me and my siblings. I love you, Saleem." He whispered. "Sometimes, I would watch you and your brothers and sisters while you were sleeping. I would just stand in the doorway and think how lucky I was."

SALEEM A. KHAN, M.D.

Saleem quietly listened to what his father had to say, until Khan Sahib shook his head, turning away from his father's grave. "There is something I want you to do for me," he said.

Saleem turned to follow.

"I would like to have my funeral service in the D Ground at the university." D Ground is a 'D' shaped park very close to the main university building.

"Okay," Saleem said, hands thrust into his pockets.

When the time came, that is exactly what his family did.

CHAPTER FIFTY-ONE

VERY FIRST HOSPITALIZATION

As he began to age, Musahib-Ud-Din had a series of minor strokes, though they could not slow him down. He kept up with things that interested him. After a severe stroke, his nephew Irshad remembered his uncle was left paralyzed on one side. Irshad rushed him to the nearest hospital. He was never hospitalized before and did not want to stay there for even an hour longer than absolutely necessary.

After a couple of days, Irshad brought his uncle home, navigating the wheelchair through the main corridor of the house. He opened the door and gently worked the wheels into the living room. He pulled a chair away from the kitchen table, opening a spot. He rolled the wheelchair up to the table so that his uncle could sit and eat his lunch.

Irshad requested the accompanying medical personnel to come inside the house. A nurse carried a heart monitoring device, and two attendants brought various self-care items, including bed railings and bathroom safety fixtures. Irshad briefly showed them around the house and left them to install the protective barriers. He joined the nurse in the living room, where she was trying to check his uncle's blood pressure and his heartbeats.

"Would you like some tea?" Irshad asked the nurse.

"Yes, please." She nodded her head.

Irshad poured the water into the teapot and turned on the stove. When the tea was ready, he offered the nurse a cup. He fixed some for the attendants who had just finished installing the bed railings and safety fixtures for the bathroom.

The nurse took her tea and sat down beside Musahib-Ud-Din. She attempted to feed the great man like a baby, but he clamped his jaw tight.

"No," he said.

"Khan Sahib," the nurse scolded.

"Leave the food on the table," he demanded. "I will eat it when I am ready."

The puzzled nurse asked Irshad for help.

"Better do what he says," Irshad told her.

The nurse sighed. She left the food near her patient, picked up her cup of tea, and left the kitchen.

"Uncle, you need to eat," Irshad stretched his hands across the table in a pleading gesture.

"I will eat it when I am hungry," he responded quickly.

Knowing it was pointless to convince him to eat, Irshad stayed quiet and walked the nurse out of the house.

CHAPTER FIFTY-TWO

TENACITY

S itting idle was not in Musahib-Ud-Din's DNA. He remained active even after his children dispersed worldwide and his wife died. When his career in government finished, he continued to make a difference in the lives of many. He mentored students at the university and paid tuition for some of them, who could not afford it because they belonged to low-income families.

One student, Mahmood, had a particularly stunning story to tell Saleem on his visit to Pakistan after his father's death. One day he invited Saleem to his office. He stood behind his chair, a leather cushioned, high-backed chair on wheels. He pulled it out from beneath the desk and gestured for Saleem to sit.

Saleem waved his hand gently, uncomfortable with the invitation.

"Please sit," the man insisted.

Saleem sat down.

Mahmood stepped around the desk and chose one of the narrow wooden chairs reserved for guests. He leaned forward, his smile wide.

"When I was young, I had only an undergraduate degree," the man said. "I was working as a junior researcher, and your father was Professor Emeritus. He was mentoring students and giving guest lectures, that kind of thing."

Saleem nodded.

"Your father would often come to my office and encourage me to return to school and get my Master's degree, but I thought I was too busy at work and could not do that. You may say I kept ignoring Khan Sahib's advice."

Saleem watched the man, clearly caught up in his memories, as his eyes drifted towards the ceiling.

"I said, 'No, no, no, Khan Sahib. I can't; I don't have the money.' Then do you know what he did? About a month later, he came to find me in my lab. He said, 'I deposited money into a university account at the registrar's office under your name. You are paid in full. Now, start working on your Master's degree.'" Mahmood sat back, opening his arms in a gesture of surprise.

Saleem leaned forward and looked at the man.

"Yes." The man nodded, "He did that."

"What did you say to my dad?" Saleem asked.

"What could I say?" The man laughed. "He had paid my tuition in full. I started attending classes and developed a plan to do relevant research. I got my Master's degree and this promotion to head of the horticulture department. It was all because of your father. The day I became the head of the department, I invited Khan Sahib and requested him to sit in this special chair first."

Tasneem, Musahib-Ud-Din's middle daughter, often told family and friends another story about her father's tenacity when he was recovering from a stroke.

In the early 1990s in Pakistan, the type of stove people generally had in their kitchens had to be lit by hand. You would turn on the gas and light a matchstick. Her father was in the habit of making morning tea, which involved lighting a matchstick to boil the water. After his stroke, his right side was relatively weak. He could get around and feed himself without assistance but he could not use both hands to light a matchstick. To solve the problem, instead of asking for help, he held the matchbox with the toes of one foot and struck the matchstick with his left hand.

One morning Tasneem found her father was having a hard time as he was trying to light a matchstick. She did not want him to struggle unnecessarily, "Father, let me do it."

"Don't be silly," her father said. "The way I am doing it works perfectly well."

At this point, his wife had already passed away, but Irshad's family was still living with him. They all offered to assist him, but he would not accept free help. Instead, he hired a lady to take care of household chores. This woman used to visit the family from time to time for years. She had come from Panipat and knew not only him and his wife but also both their extended families. She started coming over daily to do the dishes, clean the floors, and manage other routine chores at his request.

She often said, "Khan Sahib, do not worry about things getting done; I am here to take care of them. You are supposed to rest." But he would insist that he wanted to do as much around the house by himself as he could, even when it was taking him a much longer time.

After his first stroke, everyone in the family worried about his recovery. He started a physical therapy program under the supervision of a local hospital and would also do exercises at home. Three months later, his paralyzed arm began working again, and he could feed himself without assistance. A month after, his loved ones observed how his affected leg was reasonably functional. He thanked God for this improvement and told his family he did not need the visiting nurse anymore. His nephew Irshad was convinced that it was only due to his uncle's willpower that he made such a remarkable recovery.

CHAPTER FIFTY-THREE

ANOTHER HOSPITAL VISIT

A nother time when Musahib-Ud-Din had a stroke was after the death of his wife. He was in a car with Saleem and Irshad. They were in Faisalabad, on their way to court to sign some documents. Khan Sahib was acting as an executor for a friend's estate, and he had an appointment at 10 a.m. Irshad had offered to drive. Saleem came along to provide company to his father. After the meeting, they all planned to go to lunch together. They were conversing about the local marketplace when Musahib-Ud-Din began slurring his words.

Irshad looked over at his uncle, taking his eyes off the road for an instant. "Uncle?" He asked.

Saleem frowned, leaning forward from the back seat.

His father appeared to be somewhat confused.

Irshad looked at Saleem.

SALEEM A. KHAN, M.D.

Saleem was a doctor, and Irshad was well versed in health care; they both knew something was wrong. Irshad deliberately made a left turn, not speeding up but veering away from the courthouse. Saleem understood what he was doing and remained silent. Irshad continued driving until the nearest hospital reared its head over the horizon.

"Where are we going?" Musahib-Ud-Din asked his nephew, "This is not the courthouse."

"I have to make a stop," Saleem lied. "I have to speak with an old friend who works here in this hospital. It won't be long."

"Okay," his father grumbled. "We are going to be late."

"Just come with us." Irshad parked the car and reached inside to help his uncle out.

Musahib-Ud-Din waved his arms away. "Why should I come out?"

"You don't want to wait in the car." Saleem came around to his father's side, anxious. "I would like to introduce you to my friend."

"Make it quick," his father demanded.

Finally, Khan Sahib agreed and got out of his seat. He swayed, and the younger men caught him. "I'm fine," he huffed.

Saleem and Irshad hurried as fast as they could under the circumstances. They tried to convince the older gentleman to move with them without ruining their subterfuge. They burst through the front door, and Saleem waved Irshad over to the waiting room. Irshad helped his uncle into a chair and stayed with him. Saleem bulldozed through a couple of doors to find a doctor.

"Khan Sahib?" The doctor approached gently, unthreading the stethoscope from around his neck.

He looked up at his son, his eyes narrowed. "Saleem?"

Saleem inhaled. The moment of truth was upon them. "We think something may be wrong," Saleem said.

"No," his father struggled out of his seat.

"Abba, please listen." Saleem held out his hands to assist, but his father thrust the help away.

"We have an appointment in court," Musahib-Ud-Din reacted firmly.

"In court?" The doctor glanced at Irshad.

"He has some documents to sign," Irshad said.

"Oh, well," The doctor nodded, "Khan Sahib, if you would just permit me to examine you. Your son is quite worried about you. I'm sure you could reschedule your court appointment."

"I will do no such thing." He tried to walk away. "I committed to being there, and I will honor that."

"Dad, please wait." Saleem quickly grabbed his father and saved him from falling on the floor.

"Let's just take him to court," Irshad said.

"We will be back in half an hour," Saleem told the doctor. "Have a bed ready."

The doctor nodded, not entirely hiding the smile in his eyes as his patient rushed to the hospital door. They piled back into the car and drove to the courthouse. Irshad waited at the curb while Saleem helped his father into the building. They found the lawyer's office, signed the documents, and stood up to leave.

"Would you like some tea?" the lawyer asked.

"No, thank you," Saleem said.

"You seem to be in a hurry," the lawyer remarked as Saleem anxiously helped his father towards the door.

"We have another appointment," Saleem said, steering his father out into the hall.

They found Irshad waiting by the car and climbed inside. Both younger men observed him as they drove back to the hospital.

"I'm fine. Why did you come here again?" Musahib-Ud-Din questioned them as soon as he saw the hospital building from a distance.

Saleem and Irshad exchanged a glance.

They stayed quiet and pulled towards the hospital entrance. Saleem helped his father to come inside while Irshad parked the car.

"Doctors don't know as much as you believe," his father told Saleem as they navigated the hallway.

Saleem ignored this particular jab against his profession. "Mr. Musahib-Ud-Din Khan." He told the receptionist.

"Right this way." She stood and came around the desk, gesturing to a hallway. An attendant stood by to help their patient. They were shown to a room, and shortly, the doctor returned to perform an examination. When the results came in, they indicated that he had suffered a stroke affecting one side of his body.

When the excitement died down, and Musahib-Ud-Din fell asleep, Saleem began to make obligatory calls to his family members to update them on his father's condition. First, he told his older sister Naeem in Peshawar. "Father has had a stroke. He's doing fine under the circumstances. He certainly needs rest; thank God he is somewhat cooperative now." Then he called his oldest sibling, Naseem, in Maryland and shared more detailed information, including the two coerced trips to the hospital and their courthouse visit.

"How could you take him out of the hospital when you knew something was wrong?" The older brother gasped.

"How could I say 'no' to him?" Saleem responded. Some of the day's anxiety began to shake loose, and he could finally see its humor. "It would have been worse for his health to miss that appointment."

Across the oceans and many time zones away, Naseem had to agree. "Thank God it worked out, and he is getting the treatment. I appreciate you calling me. Stay in touch, please."

Musahib-Ud-Din stayed in the hospital for a week and received help from the best doctors. On every visit, the doctors encouraged him to rest as much as possible. His family came to visit him every day. Irshad and Saleem spent a lot of time with him, listening carefully to what he had to say. He would often ask them how everyone was doing in the family.

From time to time, his hospital visitors debated the corruption charges against the prime minister, Benazir Bhutto, the first female head of a Muslim country. Musahib-Ud-Din was very fond of the prime minister and supported her policies of improving the conditions of the poor people. One day he told his visitors, "I hope I get a chance to see her personally and tell her I knew her father well."

He disliked the hospital food and ate little except salad and fresh fruits. He despised the daily checkups and all the tests the doctors would order.

One day, he told Irshad, "I am supposed to be the proctor of an exam. It is scheduled for tomorrow."

"Okay." Irshad could sense rough waves on the horizon.

"Help me get up," he asked his nephew.

Irshad scrambled out of his bedside seat. "Let me get the doctor and let him know about your request to leave the hospital."

"You don't need to get the doctor," his uncle roared, but Irshad was already out of the room.

Irshad returned within a few minutes with the doctor in tow. "What is this about leaving the hospital, Khan Sahib?" The doctor pulled the chart from the foot of the bed and started reviewing it.

"I am supposed to be the proctor for an exam." Musahib-Ud-Din looked at the doctor.

"I don't think so," the doctor replied.

"Oh, but I think so," Professor Khan argued.

"Uncle, please," Irshad pleaded. "Listen to the doctor."

"No," his uncle said, "It's on my schedule. I made a commitment."

Irshad and the doctor looked at each other.

"What if I arrange for the pupils to come here?" Irshad suggested.

"That would be okay." Musahib-Ud-Din agreed.

"Yes, we could arrange for space," the doctor offered.

"Great," Irshad said. "Please wait for me. I will talk to the university officials in charge of this test."

His uncle closed his eyes, nodding quietly.

Irshad rushed from the room and drove to the university. He learned that it was a graduate-level class with only four students.

He discussed his uncle's request with the department director, who replied, "Here is the list of students. Please get in touch with them and tell them to meet your uncle at the hospital."

Irshad was able to contact each one of them. The following day, Professor Khan's pupils arrived at his hospital bed. Irshad produced the test booklets that he picked up from the university. Musahib-Ud-Din gave a short talk to his pupils before proctoring the exam. Irshad stayed to collect the test booklets and couriered them back to the university.

"Thank you so much," Irshad said to the department director.

"No problem. I am glad I could help." The director replied.

"My uncle is very appreciative of this favor."

SALEEM A. KHAN, M.D.

"Your uncle means a great deal to this department. The pupils are lucky to have him. We feel honored to accept any time he gives us." The director smiled.

CHAPTER FIFTY-FOUR
TRAVELING

After retirement, Musahib-Ud-Din spent a good deal of his time traveling. He was visiting friends and family in different parts of the country. Occasionally, he would take a trip to the U.S. to see his children and their families.

When his father came to visit him, Saleem received him at the airport. He helped his father sit comfortably in the car. Saleem felt his father was weaker now than ever before. He kept a watchful eye as he closed the car door. Then he put the luggage in the trunk and drove home. In the driveway, Saleem offered an arm to his father. Together they worked their way to the front door, where Khan Sahib received a warm welcome.

At one point, One of Musahib-Ud-Din's doctors told him that he should stop traveling by air if the trip required several hours nonstop. He was still recovering from his last stroke. The doctor felt that long air travel could be risky in his weakened condition.

One day after dinner, Saleem expressed concern about his father traveling long distances. He said, "Abba, what did your doctor say about traveling?"

"Oh, nothing," He quickly replied.

Saleem felt his father was suspiciously brief. He thought it was better to drop that matter and not ask any more questions. Only after his father returned to Pakistan and they were on the phone together did Khan Sahib confess the truth. "You asked about what my doctor said."

"Yes." Saleem sat at his kitchen table, phone in hand and bills spread before him.

"I lied," his father couldn't contain a chuckle.

"Abba, so you did not listen to your doctor?" Saleem asked.

"The doctor said I shouldn't come to the U.S."

"Father!" Saleem gasped in exasperation.

"He said I shouldn't travel by air anymore." Now Saleem's father was laughing.

"It is not funny," Saleem said.

"It *is* funny," his father argued.

"What if something happened?" Saleem was upset. "Your doctor was concerned about your well-being."

"Doctors don't know everything," Khan Sahib interrupted. "I am fine. My trip was fine. Would you prefer that I hadn't come?"

"No." Saleem swallowed his objections. "But in the future, I will come to visit you."

"And bring your whole wonderful country with you?" He teased his son.

"Father–" Saleem sighed.

"Don't worry too much about me. I am fine," Khan Sahib closed the discussion by reminding him, "I will wait for your phone call on the weekend."

CHAPTER FIFTY-FIVE

TASNEEM AND HER DAUGHTERS

Musahib-Ud-Din regularly invited his daughter Tasneem to come to stay with him during the summer and winter vacations. After her retirement, Tasneem started visiting her father more often.

She had a Master's degree in economics. After teaching for more than three decades, she retired as head of the economics department of a women's college. While his mother and wife had been deprived of education, Musahib-Ud-Din encouraged his daughters, granddaughters, and nieces to get as much education as possible. He expected scholastic achievement from them and was rewarded by many professional women in the family.

All three of Tasneem's daughters were little girls growing up in Lahore. Every year during the month of Ramadan, they would anxiously wait for their Eidee (gift on Eid) through the mail, sent by their grandfather.

They liked this special month because their mother made nice snacks and dishes every evening when their parents would break the dawn-to-dusk fast.

Mamoona, the middle daughter, woke up one day before the sunrise and saw her parents eating. She asked them, "Mom, Dad, why are you eating this early in the morning?" Her father replied, "Because it is the month of Ramadan and your mother and I keep the fast every day."

While they were talking about Ramadan, the other two girls woke up. The oldest daughter, Farah, said to her parents, "I want to keep the fast like you do."

Her mother responded, "You are not required to keep the fast, you are still a child. The fasts are from dawn to dusk, and you are not allowed to eat or drink."

At this point, Farah said, "I cannot do that, but I can try for a few hours."

"It would be good practice to help you fast all day when you grow up," Tasneem said.

The youngest daughter, Uzma, noticed that every night her father went to a neighborhood mosque. She asked her father, "Dad, why do you come home so late?"

Her father explained, "During the month of Ramadan, every night there are special prayers called Tarawih. The Imam recites from the Holy Quran. We also say the night prayer (Isha) in the mosque. Together, it takes almost two hours."

As the girls grew up, they learned a lot of facts about Ramadan and why it was considered to be a very special month.

Mamoona told her parents, "We learned in school that during the month of Ramadan, Muslims should read the Holy Quran every day and give food, clothes and money to poor people." She continued, "Our teacher said, fasting is not just abstaining from eating and drinking all day long; Muslims are supposed to do good deeds and stay away from everything bad."

The little girls learned to expect a special gift from their grandfather every year. Mamoona and her sisters would rush towards the mailman every time he cycled down the street during Ramadan.

"Do you have anything for us? Do you have anything for us?" They would chant.

"No." The mailman would smile. "Not yet. Maybe tomorrow."

Eventually, their envelope would come, and in it, a small amount of cash they could spend any way they chose. Their grandfather sent a note in the envelope, telling them to share some with the mailman. Every year when he delivered a gift to the children, the mailman also received money for his family.

"Why did you do that?" A few years later, Tasneem asked her father over a cup of tea at the kitchen table in her home when he was visiting her family in Lahore.

"Do what?" her father asked.

"Send the mailman a tip every Eid?"

He shrugged. "I'm sure he has a family, and they could use a little extra money too."

"But, have you ever met the mailman who brings mail to our neighborhood?"

He smiled, "No. But that doesn't mean he doesn't work hard. I think he deserves to have Eidee too. I am sure it makes him happy."

One summer, when Tasneem was visiting her father, they went on a walk around midday. Her father wanted to show Tasneem some new shops that had opened since she visited last.

As they approached the business district, Professor Khan spotted a food vendor and said, "This poor guy has very little money. He built a cart and started selling food he and his wife cooked themselves. But I never see many customers."

Tasneem's father approached the man and nodded politely. "Two chanay, please." Chanay is a typical Pakistani dish cooked with chickpeas, vegetables, and spices. Many people like to eat it with bread (naan) at breakfast. It can also be used as a snack.

Tasneem held her tongue, watching her father conduct the transaction. When money changed hands, and Khan Sahib accepted the bag of food, they pushed on into the city.

"Why did you buy that?" Tasneem whispered. "I can make that better for you at home." She knew well that her father did not care for cooked food sold in the market and loved home-cooked meals.

"To support the vendor," her father answered. Later that day, he gave the food to his housekeeper and ate a meal instead that his daughter had prepared.

CHAPTER FIFTY-SIX

FAMILY

F amily was always very important to Musahib-Ud-Din. He continued
to support his own extended family and that of his wife. All the
people he rescued from Partition and many of their children lived in
Faisalabad. He ensured that the clan was housed and well fed. He also paid
for several young family members' education.

Four of his children (three sons and one daughter) settled in America:
Walayet in Indiana, Saleem in Delaware, Naseem in Maryland, and
daughter Shamim in Texas. "Why don't you come stay with us?" they often
asked.

But Musahib-Ud-Din had too much of a stake in Pakistan to leave. He
regularly visited Ayub Research Institute and enjoyed discussing the latest
developments in agriculture. He had the university, where he continued to
teach. He had two daughters still in Pakistan: Tasneem and Naeem.

Shamim was the youngest daughter. She died of breast cancer when she
was 56. Her daughter, Nadia, became a family physician at the Texas Tech
University Health Science Center in Lubbock, Texas. Shamim's two sons
also settled in the U.S. Her older son, Rizwan, is a system analyst and lives

in Denver, Colorado. Her younger son, Usman, is a realtor in Houston, Texas.

Musahib-Ud-Din was Director General Ayub Agricultural Research Institute from 1973 to 1974. His nephew Dr. Noor-Ul-Islam always felt proud that he followed his uncle's footsteps and had the honor of heading the institute as Director General. He held this prestigious position from 2010 to 2013. Like his uncle, he did significant research work and published his findings in well-respected journals.

Naeem was very impressed by her father's interest in botany. After all her children became busy with school, she started taking graduate classes. She was successful in earning her Master's degree in botany. One of Musahib-Ud-Din's grandchildren, Jawad, followed in his footsteps, achieving a doctorate in soil sciences from the University of Arkansas.

Most of Professor Khan's children, like him, became educators. His grandson Tahawar (Naseem's son), did his PhD in English and for many years taught in schools in Maryland state. He felt very proud to continue the tradition of teaching, a tradition started by his great grandfather Hafiz Sher Muhammed Khan.

Many relatives have stories of Musahib-Ud-Din encouraging them to follow their dreams and obtain higher education. One by one, his children followed in his footsteps and started helping others in their educational endeavors. More than twenty years after his death, his children still support deserving students financially in the extended family.

If anything can attest to Professor Khan's emphasis on education, it is the academic achievements of his children, grandchildren, nephews, and nieces. Many of them became physicians, educators, system analysts, scientists, principals, and directors.

As much as he could, Khan Sahib also tried to help family members with their genuine needs other than education. His children wholeheartedly supported his efforts both then and now, feeling proud to continue a worthwhile tradition started by their beloved father. In the present generation of the Khan family, very few individuals need financial assistance. Some of them have actually started helping others in the family and are supporting worthy causes in the community.

CHAPTER FIFTY-SEVEN

MUNAZA

O ne thing that made an impression on many grandchildren was their grandfather's habit of taking naps in the afternoon. He stuck to his schedule. He had a penchant for healthy habits and one of his routines involved napping. When his grandchildren visited, he insisted they either nap or remain quiet. His wife liked this idea because it allowed her to rest in the middle of the day.

Munaza, Naeem's daughter, remembered parties of cousins who would not nap, tiptoeing around the house until they were caught. They laughed and hid when the grandfather got up to chastise them.

"He would laugh with us," Munaza said. "But then encourage us to go back to nap. It was fun and a little bit scandalous."

One of Khan Sahib's favorite activities with grandchildren was visiting relatives. He had relatives stationed all over Faisalabad and they would spend mornings visiting different houses. Munaza remembered some relatives in Faisalabad had grand four-story dwellings, while others lived in humble abodes. She visited her aunts and uncles who had migrated from

Panipat and was always excited to see her cousins. She had no memories of her great grandparents, Sher Muhammed and Fazalunnisa.

Munaza considered her grandfather as a confidant and close friend. "I would tell him things I wouldn't even tell my parents. I was afraid they would unnecessarily worry," she explained. "It helped me. I didn't have to keep things to myself."

During one family dinner, her grandfather startled Munaza with his bluntness. Throughout her life Munaza had been attending gender-specific schools. All her classmates had been girls in elementary school, high school, and college. When she entered medical school, suddenly the student population was mixed. Her grandfather knew this and used the information to tease his granddaughter about it.

"Munaza, you know if you like a boy, just come and let me know." He said, breaking apart a bit of bread in his hands. "If he is a real gentleman from a good family, we will have no problem."

Munaza said she dropped the food she had been holding, her jaw ratcheting open. She looked from her grandfather to her parents, horrified.

Her grandfather laughed. "You are an adult," he said. "You are studying around a lot of 'cute' guys. So just let us know."

This was not a conversation Munaza wanted to have in front of her parents. She stooped to mop up her mess, feeling her cheeks flush. Later, without her parents, she and her grandfather discussed the situation in a realistic way. She did not have a particular boy in mind, but it was fun to talk about the possibility.

Munaza's parents did not arrange her marriage in the traditional sense. After completing her medical school education, when she was under training as a resident, she had a friend with whom she was interested in getting serious with. She and her soon-to-be husband involved their parents and had the two mothers discuss the details. Although his own marriage had been arranged, and he had helped arrange marriages for his children, he was open to his granddaughter choosing her own life partner.

"I'm still very traditional," Munaza said. It was the best of both worlds. She had support from her family and the love of a good friend.

She remembers how her grandfather used to keep a copy of her exam schedule. In Munaza's school, every student was given a syllabus for every class at the beginning of each semester. They also received a sheet holding the dates of every exam and paper due in that class. Munaza used to mail a copy to her grandfather when he was living in Faisalabad and she in Peshawar. He stayed on top of it, phoning her to ask how she had performed each exam and whether she completed her projects on time.

"One day, I told him I scored 94 out of 100 on a math test," Munaza said. "And his response was, 'why didn't you score 100?' He thought that was a poor score."

With such high standards, one might think he was wound very tight, but that was not the case. Munaza remembered one exam in particular. It was at the end of high school, a very critical exam that would have real consequences for her future. Her mother had gone to America to visit her sister, leaving her teenage children home. Musahib-Ud-Din arranged to travel to Peshawar with his wife to stay with them so that the grandchildren could focus on their studies. On the evening of the test when Munaza was a bundle of nerves, her grandfather pulled her aside.

He said, "Just relax. Go on, take your test and leave the result to Allah."

CHAPTER FIFTY-EIGHT

LEGACY

O ne night, Musahib-Ud-Din called his daughter Naeem in Peshawar. His granddaughter, Munaza, picked up the phone. She was studying for her 3rd-year medical school exam. She wondered why her grandfather called so late.

"Your Grandma's death anniversary is coming up in a couple of days. You should visit me and attend it with the rest of the family."

In Pakistan, families gather once a year for many years after the passing of a loved one. In these gatherings, family and friends remember the deceased by telling one another stories about their loved ones who died. Sometimes people spend days cooking meals to feed extended family and friends, who come from all over to the deceased's home. They read from the Holy Quran and pray together for the dead. These gatherings help to maintain close ties between family and friends.

"I'm sorry, Grandpa," Munaza replied. "I have an exam coming up."

"Oh," her grandfather asked, "When is the exam?"

Previously, he had known when Munaza's exams were, but she forgot to tell him about this crucial end-of-the-year exam. "It's the day after," she said.

"Can't you come anyway?" he asked again.

"I'm sorry," she said. In the back of her mind, a tiny voice of alarm sounded, but she smothered it. Her grandfather always praised her schoolwork; why was he asking her to prioritize something ahead of her education? He was the one who inspired her to go to medical school. He often said, 'school before everything else.'

"That means I won't see you again," he said.

"I will tell Mom and Dad that you want us to visit as soon as possible. Inshallah, we will come to Faisalabad right after my exam." She said, still not understanding why her grandmother's death anniversary that year was so important.

"Okay," he said. "I will miss you."

"I will miss you too." She signed off, staring at the phone for a moment before sliding it back into its cradle. Was that weird? She wasn't sure. He had said: *I won't see you again*. His words were prophetic because shortly after his wife's death anniversary, Musahib-Ud-Din passed away.

"Several people told my mother that he was different in the last week before his death," Munaza said. "He visited all of his friends and family in Faisalabad. They all said he seemed at peace."

Professor Khan woke up one morning alone in bed. He took a shower. He preferred to shower in the evening, so he could towel off and climb into bed. But this morning, he washed off early.

He went to the university. He spoke with a few colleagues, research scientists and students. He checked his mail. There were no counseling sessions scheduled for him that day.

He stopped by one of the experimental gardens to see how the young kinnow plants were coming along. He was pleased to see the buds of a few kinnows poking out from beneath the green canopy. These fruits would outlive him. They would be one of his many legacies.

On his way back home from the university, he visited one of his nieces, Ghazala. He brought a lot of fruits for her family. He said to her, "These nice kinnows are specially for you."

Ghazala recalls he did not look well. She asked, "Are you not feeling well?" She felt he did not appear his usual cheerful self.

He was quick to respond, "I'm fine. I'm fine." Then he requested, "You must come to visit me in the morning."

Ghazala didn't want to let him go. She could see that he looked somewhat pale. She did everything she could think of to implore him to stay. But she felt he was like a force of nature and was determined to leave.

He took a rickshaw home, but instead of going inside, he went straight to his neighbor's house. According to the neighbor, he could not speak. With gestures, he conveyed to her that he was not feeling well. Then with one hand, he pointed at Ghazala's phone number.

She said, "You want me to call Ghazala?"

He nodded his head to affirm that was what he wanted.

Looking at his face, which was turning quite pale, she ran to get her husband.

"Zaheer, come quick," the woman cried, "Professor Khan needs immediate help."

Zaheer came to the door and looked at the professor's face. "Get my keys," he told his wife.

Together, the neighbors urged the elderly gentleman towards their car. They sat him down in the back seat, allowing him to recline. His breathing was labored now, sharp gasps coming at irregular intervals.

"Hurry," the woman said.

Her husband nodded, accepting the keys and leaping into the driver's seat. He sped towards the hospital, keeping an eye on Professor Khan the whole way. But it was perhaps too late when he pulled up to the emergency room entrance.

Orderlies lifted him onto a gurney and wheeled him into the hospital. A doctor came immediately. He looked at Khan Sahib's face, checked his pulse and breathing, and then told Zaheer, "I am very sorry, he has already passed away."

Ghazala rushed to the emergency room and heard the sad news. She cried, wondering how the world would ever recover from the loss of this extraordinary man.

CHAPTER FIFTY-NINE

CELEBRATING THE LIFE OF A LEGEND

T he aftermath of his death left the family in shock. Grief was something they all had experienced before, but it was particularly significant this time. His passing brought many mourners out of communities across the country.

His daughters Tasneem and Naeem and their families rushed to Faisalabad. By the time they arrived, the extended family had already washed the body and were getting ready to proceed to the D-Ground on the university campus for funeral prayers.

In Pakistan, if a loved one dies in a hospital, the body is brought home quickly, and family members wash it before the funeral prayer. According to Islamic traditions, Muslims are encouraged not to delay the burial of the deceased. Tasneem and Naeem shared the sad news with the rest of the family, including their one sister and three brothers, who were all residing in different parts of America. A steady stream of well-wishers stopped by, bringing food and sharing stories. Soon the kitchen table was full of curries, platters, and fruits.

One young man told his daughters that their father had bought him a motorcycle. "I had no way to get to my college," the young man said. "I didn't even ask him, but Khan Sahib just bought one for me."

"He helped me buy a piece of land," another gentleman said. "I built my house there, and I was able to marry and start my family. Now we have four children." He wiped tears from his eyes as he told everyone his story.

"I remember one day he was sweeping the hallway outside a classroom of our botany department." A professor commented, "I said, 'Professor Khan, why are you sweeping?' And do you know what he said?"

Naeem shook her head.

"He said, 'Someone spilled trash.' Just like that. He didn't wait for the cleaning staff; he just did it himself."

The memorial services were more extensive than anything the family could have imagined. As Khan Sahib requested, the main funeral prayer was held on the D-Ground at the University. Students and faculty, both retired and active, and their families all came. Ayub Research Institute staff were also present at his funeral service. His family felt honored that both prestigious organizations remembered him so fondly.

Saleem had already started a scholarship program at the agriculture university while his father was still alive. He wanted his father's academic excellence recognized and to give young people a chance to reach their educational dreams.

For the 40th day traditional ceremony (chehlum), when Saleem and his wife arrived at his father's residence, packing had already begun. Most of the professor's possessions were in boxes in the living room. The couch was full of pillows and blankets. No one touched his bed and its dressings so his visiting family could use them as needed.

Sabira made tea for everyone, and the guests began to pick at the nuts, fruits, and deserts on the table. Before everyone could get comfortable, there was a knock on the front door. Saleem opened it.

"Assalamu alaikum." A well-dressed gentleman stood on the front step.

"Walaikum assalam," Saleem replied.

"Who is it?" Tasneem came up behind him.

"We would like you and your family to join us for a special condolence meeting at 8 a.m. tomorrow in the main library hall of the university."

Saleem accepted the invitation from the man, who also handed over a framed photo of his father with the university logo on the back. "Thank you," Saleem said.

It was unexpected, but not unwanted. Luckily they were all there so they had an opportunity to attend the condolence meeting at the university. The guests slept in two of the unoccupied sections in the house. A few minutes before eight the next morning, they bundled up against the winter air, arriving at the university gate. There was something massive going on. Saleem could see cars parked outside the dedicated parking lot, overflowing into the yard. Some of the cars were big, expensive, and well-polished. People streamed towards the library, men in winter coats and women in sh awls.

"What is happening here?" Saleem asked the guard near the gate.

"There's an international conference. It will start at nine," the guard replied.

"Are we in the right place?" Sabira wondered, glancing around.

"Maybe we understood the time wrong," Saleem said.

While trying to figure out who could help them, a man in a dark business suit and gray tie waved his hand at them. He hurried toward the Khan family and told the guard, "This is Dr. Saleem Khan and his family. They are our special guests." He requested the family to follow him.

Saleem held his hand out to Sabira, and they walked toward the library entrance. Saleem was asking himself if he had ever met the man, was he one of his father's pupils? Surely he would remember someone who recognized him.

"I'm sorry, sir." Saleem hastened his steps to draw level with the gentleman guiding them, "Where do I know you from?"

"I was one of Professor Khan's pupils," the man said. "I am now the head of the botany department at the university. I owe that to your father. He always encouraged me to excel in my academic endeavors."

Saleem fell back a moment; here was yet another example of the kindness of the man who had so recently departed them. "Did we meet before?" Saleem tried again, still confused.

"We used to come to your house when you were a teen. My fellow students and I would come in the afternoons for guidance from your dad about our projects. You and your siblings used to bring mango juice for us. I am sure you did join us at least a couple of times." The man smiled, reaching the library door.

"We are glad to see you," Saleem said, relieved. He remembered those afternoons and the delight of listening to his father in the presence of advanced college students.

When they stepped into the library, they observed that the students' tables had been moved away. The resulting space was like a big auditorium, framed by bookshelves. Inside, ladies and gentlemen were talking in hushed tones. University professors, and directors in their business suits congregated around displays of photographs and framed writings. Many scientists and university students were also among the more than four hundred mourners seated in chairs and standing in the aisles. The amount of power and knowledge in the room was staggering.

"I never realized until just then that Dad was not only famous, he was also very popular," Saleem said.

Saleem was invited to speak when the crowd settled into their seats. With tears in his eyes, he read the Urdu poem that he had written to express his feelings of sorrow on his father's death.

Naseem's wife, Mumtaz, was a special education teacher in the U.S. She prepared a speech on behalf of the family.

"Ladies and gentlemen! We would like to thank Vice Chancellor Dr. Riaz Hussain Qurashi for organizing this befitting condolence meeting. We are gathered here to pay our tribute to the late Professor Musahib-Ud-Din Khan. He was a loving father, a dedicated scientist, and a man of great drive and energy. His dedication and devotion to promote education among the people around him were phenomenal.

SALEEM A. KHAN, M.D.

"He had an utmost love for this university. He came here as a student and ended his career as Professor Emeritus. After his retirement, he preferred to live all his life in Faisalabad to stay close to the Agriculture University and Ayub Research Institute. A few times, I had the privilege to be with him when he visited the university. How proud he was of this place was evident from his talk and his walk. I felt as if every breath he took on the premises was nourishing for his soul. My beloved father-in-law had a very keen eye for talent. He always encouraged and assisted those who exhibited an aptitude for learning. His curiosity for knowledge lasted until the end.

"My husband, Naseem Khan, the eldest son, was very close to his father. Last night from the United States over the telephone, while sobbing with grief, he paid his tribute to his father by saying,

"'I want to let thousands of his students and associates know that a wonderful, most effective, results-oriented, and principled man has moved on to his maker! And he was my father!' I wish my husband was here today to experience the love and respect being expressed for his father.

"For 36 years, I was his daughter-in-law and his great admirer. I have always admired his quest for knowledge. He encouraged me and acknowledged my talents and my achievements. He was my rock. My steadfast support. His passing away is a great loss for me.

"Ladies and gentlemen, we celebrate that he lived a beautiful, meaningful, and productive long life. We regret that all good things someday do and have to come to an end. To near and dear ones, the end always feels untimely. Today the challenge for his family, his professional colleagues, and his students is to fill the void in such a way that would be most befitting to his legacy. As you know, he leaves behind very talented sons, daughters, grandsons, granddaughters, and thousands of his students. I feel very confident they will do their best to keep making a positive difference for humanity, as he did all his life. May his soul rest in peace. Ameen."

When any of his children, grandchildren, nieces, or nephews meet agriculture scientists from Pakistan, they are amazed to discover the extent of his influence.

"In Pakistan, people always talk about him fondly," Saleem said. "It is not just in Pakistan. If we run into his students anywhere in the Middle East, Europe or North America, they tell us how they loved him and how he helped them develop professionally."

Chapter Sixty

U.S. After Half A Century

By Professor Musahib-Ud-Din Khan

In the year 2001, I visited my family in the United States. The main purpose of my visit was to attend the wedding ceremonies of my two grandsons. I spent about two months in the U.S. During this period of time, I visited several cities on the east coast and then went to Las Vegas. I also traveled to Chicago and Houston and the states of Indiana and Florida.

I visited many people from all different walks of life. I was impressed to see the progress and prosperity all around America. I admire the hard working Americans, who have done an excellent job of making their country a leader for the rest of the world. The highway system in the country is awe-inspiring. I like the fact that most people do their assigned tasks with enthusiasm and honesty. In my opinion, Americans are very reliable, they have a high sense of accountability, and their problem-solving skills are quite advanced. Because of all these qualities of people, the country has been a world leader.

I found people on the streets and in supermarkets to be courteous. At one airport, I had to wait for a couple of hours because of a delay in our flight. I wanted to inform my family about this change. I was looking around for a public phone. In the meantime, a gentleman walked up to me and offered his cell phone for me to use.

I bought a few clothes in Houston. When I was in Indiana visiting my son, I felt like returning a couple of them. My son took me to a store of the same name in his town. Without any hesitation, they took the clothes back. I do not know of such an efficient system in other parts of the world.

Most countries have one or two airlines, but in the U.S., I was amazed to see so many companies operating. It seemed that air travel was the most typical way people traveled from one place to another in the country.

I visited several Pakistani families. They appeared to be happy and content with their lives. Many were satisfied with President George W. Bush and his administration. One of my children is a big supporter of President Bush. He wrote a letter to the President admiring his tax reduction initiative. Also, he praised the policy of supporting the social service work performed by religious organizations. I was delighted to learn that my son received a signed thank you letter from President Bush.

Wherever I visited, as an agriculture scientist, I paid particular attention to plants, fruits, and food products. I was hoping to see fresh fruits and vegetables in the supermarkets, but that was not always the case. I saw a lot of greenery on the east coast. Still, when I was in the Las Vegas area, the trees did not look as green (perhaps because of the strong heat during

August in that part of the country). In Nevada, the climate is such that date plants can be easily grown. I wonder why it has not been done yet?

In 1951 and 1952, when I was doing my research work at the University of California, Berkeley, food preservation was a field in its infancy. Almost half a century later, when I returned, It appeared to me that things had gone full circle. People seemed to be more interested in fresh fruits and vegetables. I certainly consider this a healthy trend.

I came to America in the early fifties for higher education and training. What I learned then was instrumental in my professional and personal growth. I understand thousands of students from all over the world come every year to the U.S. to learn about the latest scientific research and advancements in every field. Based on what I saw during my recent visit to this great land of freedom and opportunities, I can confidently predict that after another fifty years, America will still be leading the rest of the world.

CHAPTER SIXTY-ONE

AGRICULTURAL PRACTICES AROUND THE GLOBE

(Translated from a brief autobiography written by Professor Musahib-Ud-Din Khan in Urdu)

I had the opportunity to visit several different countries. Wherever I visited, I observed agricultural practices and wrote about them in Pakistani magazines and newspapers.

Japan: I was told that for agriculture graduates to advise farmers, they had to work in multiple branches of agriculture and pass a national exam. The students who chose to study agriculture sciences, from the beginning they were involved in practical hands-on work. Japan is advanced in many ways. I saw people growing vegetables using mineral solutions. Wherever we visited in Japan, we were served tea without sugar or milk.

Philippines: I visited the rice research center located outside of Manila. They were studying all aspects of rice. I learnt that Pakistani scientists were regularly visiting the institute. I liked seeing the gardens of pineapples. I observed bananas and mangoes; they were growing on small hills. After seeing them, I was convinced that it is true that the climate is more important than the soil for cultivation of fruits.

Thailand: I went to see an international maize research center. They kept corn (maize) seed in cold storage, at a special temperature for the best results. They showed us an insect that was eating up the insects that destroy corn. As such, they felt no need to spray insecticide on their corn plants.

Egypt: I attended a meeting organized by F.A.O. (Food and Agriculture Organization), a branch of the United Nations. An Egyptian agriculture specialist told me that the climate of Egypt was suitable for the cultivation of cotton. All the farmers living in a village were coordinating the planting, spraying and picking of cotton. This collaborative approach was helpful for them when it came time to send their cotton to the packaging factories. I was told every cotton processing factory had a representative from the agriculture department of the government, who made sure the quality and packaging practices were up to international standards. I also tasted the Naval oranges which were excellent . This variety did not do well in Pakistan.

Iran: In Iran, I visited the Agriculture Institute. Their labs were equipped with modern instruments and gadgets. I liked how in the chemistry lab, they would put fresh samples of crops in a machine and receive details of the ingredients. In the market, I saw oranges from Turkey, Lebanon and

Israel. Pakistani Kinnows were very popular there. Their own oranges were bitter in taste.

Lebanon: I fell in love with this country for its beauty. On the seaside I saw banana and date trees, while the hilly side areas grew high quality apples. Outside Beirut, I visited a citrus packing plant. First, they rejected the bad fruits, then washed and waxed the remaining lot. As the last step, the fruits were wrapped around with paper and then put in boxes for export. When I met with the Director of Agriculture, Mustafa Zahoor, he told me that Lebanon had increased the production of vegetables and fruits for export purposes.

Europe: I visited Germany and France. They were using the latest technology. In Germany, I noticed they were cutting their crops in such a way that significant portions of the plants were left on the ground. This approach helped them avoid green fertilizers. In France, I was very impressed by their sophisticated canal irrigation system. They were using electric power to bring water from a river to the canals. This system of irrigation was quite effective for the cultivation of rice.

USA: I visited this progressive country several times. The country was growing all kinds of grains and many varieties of vegetables and fruits. I observed research going on all the time to improve the quality and quantity. I visited a few agriculture research institutes and discussed the pioneering work of their scientists. It was quite a learning experience for me. I felt America was rightfully the world leader in many fields.

CHAPTER SIXTY-TWO

MEMORIES OF MY FATHER

"Abba, why are you standing outside my school? I know President Ayub Khan is visiting the Agriculture Institute today." My father calmly replied that he had come to the school to check if my math test for the final exam went well. He was concerned that I would be very upset if I did not do well on my test. I have many such memories of my father's dedication and commitment to his children and their education.

Among his family and friends, he was one of the few fathers who encouraged their daughters to receive higher education. My two sisters and I obtained graduate degrees and were very successful in our careers. I think his commitment to education stemmed from the fact that from a humble background, he had the opportunity to get an education in very prestigious institutions. He always told us it was education that enabled him to become successful in life.

He was very invested in creating educational and learning opportunities for others. After he retired from the government, he devoted much of his time translating the latest international research into Pakistan's national language, Urdu, so that ordinary people could learn about scientific advancements.

After my marriage, he supported my decision to be a stay-at-home mother and raise my four children. Once all my children were in school, I decided to teach biology to high school students. He supported that decision wholeheartedly. In my teaching career, I stayed true to the work ethic I learned from my father. Besides many other things he also taught us the virtue of helping others. The values I learned from my father, I always taught them to my children and my students.

He held himself to the highest standards of ethics as a government officer. He never gave in to the pressure from politicians or other influential individuals. He always did what was right legally and morally and what was in the best interest of Pakistan.

My father had complete faith in his abilities. No defeat or challenge could discourage him or affect his optimism. He would invariably come back with a plan and achieve his goals with a strong faith in Allah, hard work, and dedication. He suffered from strokes a few times. Once even doctors gave up on him. However, with his willpower, he pushed himself and started intensive physical therapy. This is how he was able to regain most of his motor functioning. I always admired his ability to fight against the odds and turn adversities into opportunities.

My husband often says that those individuals who followed my father's advice were very successful professionally and served their communities well. As much as I appreciate all his achievements, they would not have been possible without my mother's unwavering support. I always felt she sacrificed a lot so her husband could follow his dreams and achieve his goals.

SALEEM A. KHAN, M.D.

Naeem Anwar Khan

MSc Botany

Biology teacher

CHAPTER SIXTY-THREE
MEMORIES OF MY GRANDFATHER

Me at age six sitting with grandpa at Mangla Dam

M y grandfather was a family-oriented and hardworking man. He excelled in his academic fields and was able to utilize that success to obtain distinguished government positions. Because of his efforts, his family members were able to achieve success in their own ways. I remember him as a jovial patriarch, a caring and nurturing man who wanted the best for his family.

SALEEM A. KHAN, M.D.

This photograph is of great significance for my family as it shows four generations of first-born males of the Khan lineage.

SALEEM A. KHAN, M.D.

My great grandfather, Sher Muhammad Khan in the chair.

My grandfather, Musahib-Ud-Din Khan standing on the left.

My father, Naseem A. Khan standing on the right.

Me, Tahawar A. Khan standing next to my great grandfather.

Another thing that makes this group special is that we are all teachers by profession and are proud to be so. I would conclude by paying my regards to my beloved grandfather.

Dr. Tahawar Ali Khan

CHAPTER SIXTY-FOUR

MEMORIES OF MY GRANDFATHER

O ne day while I was walking with my grandfather, a car stopped near us. A couple of gentlemen came out to pay respect to him. When they left, I asked him, "Abba, you don't feel embarrassed that you go to university on a bicycle while others drive nice cars?"

He said, "No, I don't feel embarrassed riding a bike to the campus. I am thankful to Allah that I can still ride a bike and do not have to depend on a car and a driver. As you know, bike riding is a good exercise too."

Abba had his first stroke when I was in his house in Faisalabad. He came back from the university and seemed angry. He went to his room to change. After a while, he came out with a shirt over his head and asked me to help as he could not move one of his arms. I helped him with the shirt, and we walked to the nearest hospital. The doctor told him he had to stay at the hospital. He insisted that he felt okay and that the arm would improve with time. Besides that, he told the doctor that he had to teach a class the next day. The doctor responded that he could not allow him to leave as he needed proper treatment immediately.

SALEEM A. KHAN, M.D.

Pretty soon, the word got out, and relatives started gathering at the hospital. He was very confident, telling everyone that he was fine and that they should not worry about him. But when his twin brother, Misbah-Ud-Din came into the room, he could not keep his composure anymore. He started crying when he looked at his brother. That made his brother cry too.

During summer vacation every year, I used to visit my grandparents. In the morning, Abba and Amman would get up, perform Fajr (morning prayer) and go for a walk. After the walk, they would come home and start making breakfast. All that time, I would still be sleeping.

One day he told me a joke about two lazy guys.

Two lazy guys were sleeping under a tree. When they got up in the morning, one of them said: "During the night, a few grapes fell on my chest, and no one had the courtesy to put them in my mouth."

The other guy said: "All night, a stray dog kept licking my face, but no one had the courtesy to chase the dog away."

Jawad Khan, PhD

CHAPTER SIXTY-FIVE

MEMORIES OF MY UNCLE

I t has been many years since my uncle passed away, but I still often think about his legacy. It is hard to find such a kind and loving person like him. In the family, we remember him as the guardian angel, who positively influenced everyone's lives, including mine.

He believed that education was the only way to change one's life for good. That is why he encouraged every child in the family to continue their schooling despite financial challenges. It became his mission to see his family members succeed in life. To fulfill his mission, he worked hard and removed financial barriers for many in the family.

Because of his incredible help and encouragement, we now have successful engineers, doctors, scientists, professors, and IT specialists in the family. They are doing remarkably well in their professions. They are undoubtedly great role models for many and offer hope for the future generations.

My uncle's kindness was not limited to just his family. His generosity touched anyone who walked into his life. One day my uncle was riding a

SALEEM A. KHAN, M.D.

rickshaw. When he found out that the rickshaw was not in good condition, he helped the driver to get it fixed so that he could have a reliable source of income. People still talk about how he helped them in so many ways when they faced stressful and desperate situations.

May Allah bless his soul and grant him a special place in His Paradise, Ameen.

Touqir Khan

Ayub Research Institute

CHAPTER SIXTY-SIX

MEMORIES OF MY GRANDFATHER

As a child, I was afraid of my grandfather because someone in the family told me he could get angry quickly. But pretty soon, I found out how he loved all of us grandchildren so much. He would often play with us and tell us riveting stories. I remember one of the stories he told: "Once in a math test, I got 120 out of 100 points." He appeared very serious.

I asked, "How is that possible, Grandpa?"

He responded, "Our teacher gave us 12 math problems and said we could answer any 10 of them. We could earn 10 points for each correct answer. I answered all twelve correctly, so the teacher gave me 120 points. He was very impressed and told the class about it too." At that point, we all started laughing, and he laughed with us.

Graduating from high school was considered sufficient education at the time. Students were given a letter of recommendation. In his letter, his school headmaster wrote, "He can be a good clerk." Around then, it was

British rule in India. They did not like Indians to have higher education. They wanted young people to learn just enough to run the daily operations of the government appropriately.

I clearly remember when my grandfather lost the function of one hand because of a stroke, and his wife, my grandmother, also passed away. He dealt with those challenges with courage, patience, and faith. He taught us that with a positive attitude and strong faith, we could handle the most challenging problems in life.

Thinking about his legacy, it is obvious to me that he will be remembered for making a positive difference in the lives of others. He would spend the least amount of money on himself. Once, he learned that a young couple in the family had trouble with their washing machine. They did not ask him for help, but to their surprise, he gave them money for a new one anyway.

One day I noticed he was wearing torn shoes. Despite all my begging and pleading, he refused to buy a new pair. Several people in his town told us that he would not think twice about helping the individuals and families who were in need. From his example, we learned to help others as much as possible.

He would often say, "Always make a serious effort to learn new things every day and stay focused on your education. This approach can be beneficial in lifting you out of poverty. Also, it can be instrumental in your success in anything you choose to do in your life."

Dr. Aliya Khan, D.D.S

Moorestown Smile Center

New Jersey

CHAPTER SIXTY-SEVEN

MEMORIES OF MY GRANDFATHER

During one summer vacation, we visited our grandparents in Faisalabad. One day, Grandpa gave me a bucket of water and a couple of rags. He asked me to go out and clean the car. Once I was done cleaning, I came inside very tired and hungry. I asked Grandma to make something for me to eat. While waiting for the food, Grandpa asked me, "So what is easier, getting an education or cleaning cars?"

I right away said, "Getting an education." This was his way of teaching me a valuable lesson that changed my life. Since that day, working hard for my education and my job has never felt like a burden.

Once I was hanging out with my friend Sheraz, at his house. The topic of universities came up. I told him, my grandfather Musahib-Ud-Din Khan was a Professor Emeritus of horticulture at the Agriculture University Faisalabad. He said that his name rang a bell. He got up, grabbed his uncle's dissertation from the bookshelf, and showed me the page where Grandfather had signed that dissertation.

SALEEM A. KHAN, M.D.

My friend commented, "Your grandfather's signature is unique."

I told him he signed with his left hand since he had a stroke and could not write with his right hand. It was a proud moment for me, realizing that no matter where I was in Pakistan, Grandfather's students made positive contributions to society.

When I was studying in America, one saying that came to my mind frequently was: "Naami koi baghair mushaqqat nahi hua." It roughly translates to: "No glory without hard work." Grandfather often used that saying to motivate us.

Rizwan Toor

System Analyst

Denver, Colorado

CHAPTER SIXTY-EIGHT
MEMORIES OF MY UNCLE

M y uncle was always kind and helpful to others. He was undoubtedly an excellent guide to me as well as his staff. I will always remember him for his love and kindness; he treated me like his own son. I saw him helping poor and deserving people all the time. He was instrumental in finding jobs for quite a few individuals. He would go out of the way to help those who could not afford to pursue their education. He was very well respected for his professional knowledge, positive attitude, and extraordinary ability to deal with challenges.

One day my uncle found out I was visiting my maternal grandfather. At that time, he was Director General of the Pakistan Agriculture Research Council and was residing in Islamabad. He sent his driver to bring me to his office. From there, he took me to Pearl Continental, where he had to reserve rooms for some foreign visiting scientists. Afterward, we went to his home and enjoyed a lovely meal with Auntie. Later he asked the driver to drop me back at my grandfather's house. I was so happy to see him and my auntie; we had a delightful time together.

SALEEM A. KHAN, M.D.

One day, when I was visiting one of my aunts, my uncle showed up. My aunt was complaining that her fridge was not functioning. Uncle listened to her but did not say much. The next day, sure enough, she had a new refrigerator. My aunt was so happy and excited to receive the unexpected gift.

Over the years, I heard several stories from different family members talking about his generosity and willingness to go out of the way to help others.

Dr. Jehanzeb Khan

Professor of History

Faisalabad, Pakistan

CHAPTER SIXTY-NINE

MEMORIES OF OUR MOHSIN (BENEFACTOR)

My father died when I was young. My Khala Wazir Begum (maternal aunt) and Khaloo Musahib-Ud-Din Khan (husband of my Khala) raised my older brother and me. They also helped my mother, who had chronic medical problems. I feel strongly that my brother and I received higher education and became successful professionals because of his guidance. My Khaloo always encouraged my sons (Bilal and Owais) to study hard and be on top of their classes. He would reward them for perfect scores on their tests. I firmly believe that my son Owais became a physician and my son, Bilal, an information technology expert because of his ongoing encouragement.

He was undoubtedly a moral man. One day, along with a friend, I took a day off to get something important done in a government office. My Khaloo accompanied us to the office. Our task ended earlier than expected. After that, my friend and I wanted to go home and enjoy the rest of the day. But my Khaloo told us to return to school and help our students with their studies and projects.

He kept his needs to a minimum. Once I told him to buy new clothes for Eid. He said he was fine wearing his old clothes. When I offered to get him a new outfit, his response was, "If we control our expenses, only then can we help those in real need." He always tried his best to help poor relatives in the family. At times, he would also help poor people in the community.

He loved his wife a lot and was always concerned about her well-being. They were together for more than half a century. It was tough for him to take her death. At her funeral, he kissed her forehead and said, "She was a very pious lady. I always respected her and admired her devotion to the family."

I pray that my Khaloo and Khala are granted a special place in the paradise, Ameen (amen)

Ghazala Raees, M.Ed

School Principal

Faisalabad, Pakistan

CHAPTER SEVENTY

MEMORIES OF KHAN SAHIB

Afterⁿ graduating from high school, I got admission to the Agriculture College Lyallpur (now Faisalabad). Professor Musahib-Ud-Din Khan was the warden of my assigned hostel. That was the first time I got a chance to see him personally. Right away, I felt he was a very caring person.

We were poor as we had just migrated from India, and the family still had trouble making ends meet. On the first day, Khan Sahib visited my room and noticed that my charpai (cot) had no bedsheet on it. He went home and brought a brand new one for me.

In those days, each student was required to bring twenty kilos of wheat flour and two kilos of Ghee every year before starting our classes. But being poor, I could not. Khan Sahib requested the gentleman in charge of the kitchen to let me dine free.

These two examples clearly show the best of Khan Sahib's kind nature. I remember he was so benevolent; he always helped people around him. He

SALEEM A. KHAN, M.D.

was a simple and magnificent soul. May Allah his soul rest in peace, and may He shower His mercy on him! Ameen.

M Tahir Saleem PhD

Editor

Farming Outlook

Islamabad, Pakistan

CHAPTER SEVENTY-ONE
HOW I REMEMBER PROFESSOR MUSAHIB-UD-DIN

M any students who graduated from Punjab Agriculture College Lyallpur served the community at large in leadership positions. Some of them were responsible for innovative ideas and discoveries that significantly helped the country. Professor Musahib-Ud-Din was certainly one of those exceptional individuals. Over many years of his professional life, he enjoyed a reputation as a superb horticulturist, a remarkable botanist, a pioneering fodder specialist, a respected soil scientist, and an extraordinary administrator.

My first encounter with Professor Musahib-Ud-Din was in 1956 when I was a 4th-year student at the college. He taught us an advanced course: 'Botany of Crop Plants.' Later on, while working on my master's degree, I benefited greatly from his lectures on genetics and plant breeding. His lessons were explicit and very interesting. This is why, after 67 years, I still remember that the rows of kernels in a corn cob are always an even

SALEEM A. KHAN, M.D.

number. His dedication to his professional work and sincere desire to help everyone earned him much respect from students, researchers, and the teaching staff.

In 1958, I joined the Botany Department and started teaching under his supervision. In 1961, along with him, I moved to the Agriculture Research Institute. Together we produced many research works. We wrote booklets entitled: *Elements of Genetics* and *Elements of Plant Breeding*. We also wrote a laboratory guide covering these subjects' practical work. We published a research paper on the cytogenetics of the Bajra x Napier Grass hybrid. We are also co-authors of a chapter on the improvement of horticultural crops in the textbook *Horticulture*. This textbook is taught to students in all the agriculture universities of Pakistan.

What I learned from him was very helpful throughout my life. He taught me how to create question papers, conduct examinations, draft official correspondence, and write scientific research papers. I developed a fondness for him because of his extraordinary knowledge, incredible teaching skills, and amiability of character. To me, he was a father figure, a superb guide, a selfless benefactor, and an exemplary human being.

Dr. Habib-Ur-Rehman

Professor of Agriculture

CHAPTER SEVENTY-TWO

LIFETIME ACHIEVEMENTS

ACADEMIC HONORS

- Sir Lewis Dane Gold Medal (First Position in BSc) 1938

- Broke Record in MSc Horticulture Honors 1943

- Master's degree (Food Science) University of California, Berkeley 1952

- Educator for 32 years

RECOGNITIONS/AWARDS

- Gold medal (Rotary International)

- Gold medal (Punjab Cooperative Fruit Development Board)

- Silver medal - Student Orator - Punjab Agriculture College

SALEEM A. KHAN, M.D.

- Member Board of Advisors, American Horticulture Institute

- Vice President Punjab Cooperative Fruit Development Board

ADMINISTRATIVE POSITIONS HELD

- Head of Botany Department Agriculture College, Faisalabad

- Director Soil Fertility, West Pakistan

- Director General Ayub Agriculture Research Institute, Faisalabad

- Head of Pakistan Agriculture Research Council

RESEARCH WORK

- Discovered beta carotene in grapefruits

- Developed a new fodder, Bajra Napier Grass (Hybrid)

- Improved mango side grafting technique

- Initiated or supervised many research projects

PUBLICATIONS

- Many professional publications based on research

- A few dozen science articles of general public interest

- Book, *Our Fodders,* about fodders of Pakistan

- Book, *Our Fruits,* about fruits of Pakistan

- Instruction manual for soil testing

- Contributed to professional books and journals

COUNTRIES VISITED

- USA

- UK

- France

- Germany

- Japan

- Iran

- Saudi Arabia

- Egypt

- Lebanon

- UAE

- Philippines

- Thailand

CHAPTER SEVENTY-THREE

WORDS OF WISDOM FROM PROFESSOR KHAN

EDUCATION

- Try to get the highest possible education despite all challenges.

- Education enables you to take advantage of opportunities.

HARD WORK

- No one ever became a success without hard work

- With hard work, you can achieve your goals easily.

HELPING OTHERS

- Your help can make a huge difference in the lives of others.

- Help others without expecting anything in return.

FAITH

- Do your best and leave the results to Allah (God).

- Keep your faith strong while facing the odds against you.

RELATIONSHIPS

- Family relations should be your top priority.

- When you treat others with respect, they will respect you.

HEALTHY HABITS

- Go out for daily walks to stay healthy.

- Have a good breakfast and take a nap every afternoon.

CHAPTER SEVENTY-FOUR

OPINIONS OF INTERNATIONAL SCIENTISTS

Dr. A. M. Boyce, Director of Citrus Experiment Station, Riverside, California

"Musahib-Ud-Din Khan is a very brilliant man and is well informed about our citrus conditions."

※※※※※ ※※※※※

Howard Scott Gentry, Botanist Plant Introduction, U.S.D.A.

"Knowing the competence of your hand and head is a pleasure."

※※※※※ ※※※※※

W. V. Cruises, Professor of Food Technology, University of California

"He is an exceptionally capable student and has done well in his research towards his M. S. Degree."

❦

E. D. Lucas, Ex-Principal Forman Christian college and member of the Committee on Friendly Relations Amongst Foreign Students, New York.

"He has made an excellent record here, both as a student and as a man of sterling character and cooperative attitude. His teachers have spoken very highly of him."

❦

S. B. Lal Singh, Fruit Specialist, Punjab

"Personally, I have a very high opinion of Mr. Musahib-Ud-Din Khan. He stood first in all classes throughout his college career. I know he won many scholarships and broke the MSc (honors) record."

CHAPTER SEVENTY-FIVE
TAHAWAR ALI KHAN'S POEM

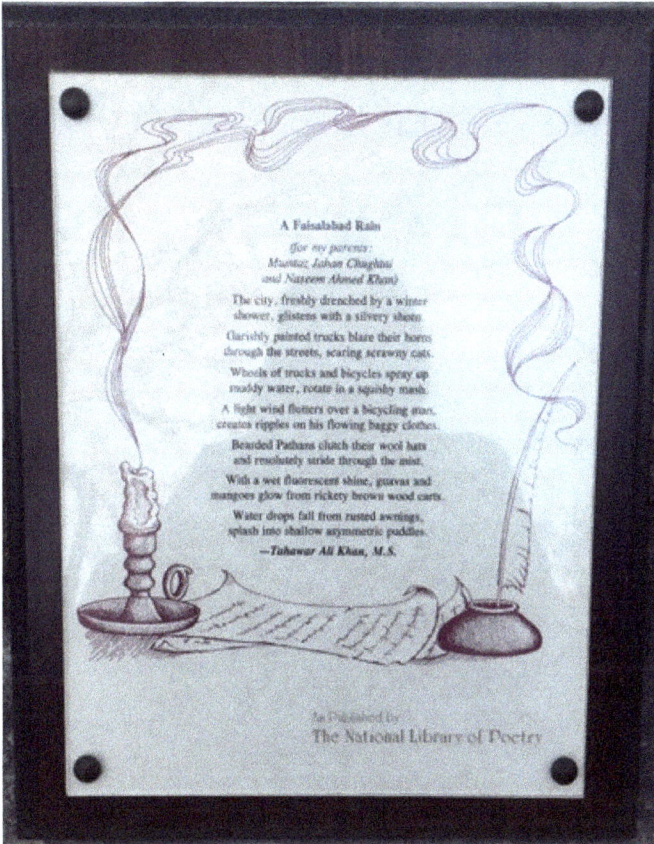

A Faisalabad Rain

(for my parents:
Mumtaz Jahan Chughtai
and Naseem Ahmed Khan)

The city, freshly drenched by a winter
shower, glistens with a silvery sheen.
Garishly painted trucks blare their horns
through the streets, scaring scrawny cats.

Wheels of trucks and bicycles spray up
muddy water, rotate in a squishy mush.
A light wind flutters over a bicycling man,
creates ripples on his flowing baggy clothes.

Bearded Pathans clutch their wool hats
and resolutely stride through the mist.
With a wet fluorescent shine, guavas and
mangoes glow from rickety brown wood carts.

Water drops fall from rusted awnings,
splash into shallow asymmetric puddles.

—Tahawar Ali Khan, M.S.

As Published by
The National Library of Poetry

Tahawar was visiting Faisalabad, the favorite city of his grandfather. One day he went to a bazaar with his grandfather and it started raining. It was that time which inspired him to create this masterpiece of a poem. It has been published by The National Library of Poetry.

CHAPTER SEVENTY-SIX

NASEEM KHAN'S POEM

East has hunger

West its loneliness

Both are hungers

One more obvious than the other

I wanted to live a little

Where do I go now?

❦

On a table talk one day, Khan Sahib asked his eldest son, "Naseem, you have been living in the US for quite some time now. What is your opinion about this country?" Naseem replied, "Abba, this land is a land of opportunity. I have no doubt about it. For my reflections on the cultures of both the US and Pakistan, I have composed a little poem. It says it all." Then Naseem read his poem to his dad.

Chapter Seventy-Seven

THAT KISS

That special kiss,

It caught me by surprise.

It was not on my head,

Actually I felt it on my cheek.

The mouth on my face,

It had no teeth.

The face was familiar,

But the action was not.

It was a surprise gift for me,

That made me stop and think.

I thought it had special meanings,

But I could not fully grasp them.

I still remember that goodbye,

At the airport in his town.

We both tried to smile,

As we were wiping our tears.

That was a kiss, from my mentor,

Who is in fact my real life hero.

I look up to him and seek his guidance,

He is no one else but my beloved dad.

Written by son Saleem after visiting his father

CHAPTER SEVENTY-EIGHT
URDU POEM

چراغِ سحری

ہمارے راستوں میں جب اندھیرے آئے
اُس چراغ سے روشنی مانگی ہم نے
آج کہاں ہے وہ چراغِ سحری؟
کیا وہ بُجھ گیا ہمیشہ کے لیے؟

وہ کیسا چراغ تھا جو بُجھ گیا
مگر ہر سُوا اسکی روشنی نظر آئے

تیری روشنی تیری تحریروں میں ہے
تیری روشنی تیری کتابوں میں ہے
تیری روشنی تیرے شاگردوں میں ہے
تیری روشنی تیری اولادوں میں ہے

تیری روشنی اک صدقہ جاریہ ہے
جو یہاں بھی ہے اور سمندروں پار بھی

تیری روشنی مشعلِ راہ بنی رہے گی
سب آنے والی نسلوں کے لیے
تیری روشنی روشن کرتی رہے گی
سب چھوٹے بڑے چراغوں کو

اے چراغِ سحری!
خدا تیری لحد کو بھی یوں جگمگا دے
جیسے اُس نے تیری زندگی کو روشن کیا تھا

۲ دسمبر ۲۰۰۱
بمطابق ۱۴ رمضان ۱۴۲۲ ہجری
(اپنے والد بزرگوار پروفیسر معاصب الدین خان کی وفات پر اُنکے بیٹے
سلیم احمد خان نے اپنے جذبات کے اظہار میں یہ الفاظ قلمبند کیے)

❦❦❦❦❦❦ ❦❦❦❦❦

Written by son Saleem to express his sorrow after his father's death.

CHAPTER SEVENTY-NINE

TIMELINE

- 1917 - Musahib-Ud-Din born

- 1932 - Graduated from high school

- 1934 - Graduated from junior college

- 1938 -Received Bachelor's degree in agriculture

- 1939 - Got married; Second World War began

- 1941 - Became a father for the first time

- 1943 - Received first Master's degree

- 1947 - Pakistan won its independence; Partition from India

- 1951 - Traveled to US to study at Berkeley

- 1955 - Accepted the responsibility as professor of botany

- 1961 -Joined Ayub Research Institute as fodder botanist

- 1966 - Appointed Director Soil Fertility West Pakistan

- 1971 - East Pakistan separated and became Bangladesh

- 1973 - Took over as Director General Ayub Institute

- 1974 - Became head of Pakistan Agriculture Research Council

- 1976 - Retired and began teaching as professor emeritus

- 1996 - Lost his wife

- 2001 - Went back to his Creator

CHAPTER EIGHTY

FAMILY TREE

PARENTS

    1. Hafiz Sher Muhammed Khan (father)

    2. Fazalunissa Begum (mother)

SIBLINGS

    1. Misbah-Ud-Din Khan (twin brother)

    2. Meraj Begum (sister)

    3. Taj Muhammed Khan (brother)

CHILDREN and GRANDCHILDREN

Naseem (son)

1. Tahawar (grandson)

2. Erum (granddaughter)

Naeem (daughter)

1. Jawad (grandson)

2. Sadia (granddaughter)

3. Aliyah (granddaughter)

4. Munaza (granddaughter)

Saleem (son)

1. Mona (granddaughter)

2. Ali (grandson)

Tasneem (daughter)

1. Farah (granddaughter)

2. Mamoona (granddaughter)

3. Uzma (granddaughter)

Shamim (daughter)

1. Nadia (granddaughter)

2. Rizwan (grandson)

3. Usman (grandson)

SALEEM A. KHAN, M.D.

<u>Walayet (son)</u>

1. Zeryab (grandson)

2. Zonair (grandson)

GREAT GRANDCHILDREN

Rimsha, Anisa, Humza

Amir, Sabrina, Danyal

Zakir, Zohair, Mueez

Usma, Usman, Raeda

Arif, Sofia, Zara, Aiza

Rayyan, Mahum, Rayyan

GLOSSARY

A bba—Father (sometimes the word is used for grandfather)

Alhamdulillah—Thank God

Allah—God

Allah Ho Akbar—God is the greatest

Ameen—Amen

Amman—Mother (sometimes the word is used for grandmother)

Assalamu alaikum—Peace be with you

Bismillah—In the name of God

Caliph—Chief Muslim civil and religious ruler

Chanay—A type of chickpeas

Charpai—Cot

Chehlum—40th day after someone's death

Eid—Celebration after Ramadan (Muslim month of fasting)

SALEEM A. KHAN, M.D.

Eidee—A gift, usually money given to children on Eid

Faisalabad—A city in Pakistan

Fajr—Morning prayer

Ghee—Clarified butter made from the milk of a buffalo or cow

Hadith—Traditions or sayings of Prophet Muhammad (PBUH)

Hajj—(Pilgrimage) Once during their lifetime, every Muslim who is physically and financially able to handle it, is required to visit the holy Sites of Mecca and Arafat during a specific time of the year.

Halal—Approved (Mostly the word is used to mean an animal approved for eating)

Henna—Plant based dye used for decoration of the skin

Imam—One who leads a prayer

Inshaallah—God willing

Jannah—Heaven

Kaaba—Most sacred site in Islam. It is considered the 'House of God' by Muslims around the world. It is the direction of prayer for them. It is located in Mecca

Kebab—Dish made of pieces of meat, roasted or grilled

Khala—Maternal Aunt

Khaloo—Maternal uncle (husband of Khala)

Khan Sahib—Respected Mr. Khan

334

Khutba—Sermon, delivered specially at Friday prayer

Mangla Dam—A dam in Pakistan located at the village of Mangla

Mehar—A gift that the groom agrees to give to his bride

Mosque—Also called Masjid, a building for worship for Muslims

Moshin—Benefactor

Nan—Oven baked flat bread

Nana—Maternal grandfather

Nani—Maternal grandmother

Nikah—A religious ceremony for a Muslims couple to be legally wed

Pakistan Zindabad—Long live Pakistan

PBUH—Peace be upon him

Qarz-e-Hasna—Interest free loan

Qibla—Direction towards the Kaaba in the sacred mosque in Mecca. It is the direction of prayers for Muslims

Quran—The sacred book of Muslims

Raja—Prince or chief

Ramadan—The month of fasting for Muslims

Rickshaw—Scooter driven small cab

Rukhsati—Sending off ceremony, when the bride leaves her home with her groom for the first time

Rupees—Unit of currency in Pakistan and India

Sufi—Someone who practices Sufism

Sufism—It is a form of Islamic mysticism that emphasizes introspection and spiritual closeness with God

Surah—A chapter in the Quran

Surah Al-Fatiha—The first Surah of Quran

Surah Al-Ikhlas—Very popular Surah that speaks to the belief in Oneness of God and that there is no one like Him

Tarawih—Special prayers during the month of Ramadan

Tanga—Horse drawn vehicle

Urdu—Pakistan's official language

Walaikum assalam—Peace be with you too

Wickets—A set of stumps used in the game of Cricket

Wudu—Ablution. Cleansing ritual for Muslims before every prayer

Zakat—Charity. The Muslims are supposed to give 2.5 percent of their surplus wealth every year to the poor and needy

CPSIA information can be obtained
at www.ICGtesting.com
Printed in the USA
JSHW012128280423
41028JS00004B/176

9 798987 787342